LIFESKETCH

4 Easy Steps to Collecting The Stories That Matter Most

By Carla Whitacre Mayer

Illustrations by Frank Ramspott

Family Memories Matter, LLC
Wheaton, Illinois
www.familymemoriesmatter.com

FAMILY
MEMORIES MATTER

This book is dedicated to Sue Lindberg
and the volunteers at
The Hemingway Birthplace Museum
who show the world how to tell a family story that combines
good research with humor and insight.

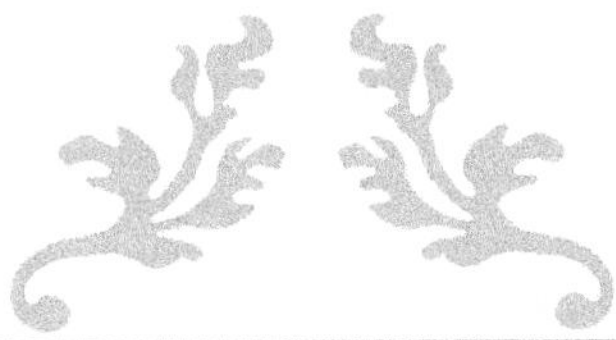

THIS BOOK BELONGS TO

If lost please contact me at…

ULTIMATELY,
WRITING FAMILY STORIES
IS AN ACT OF LOVE –
LOVE FOR THOSE WHO CAME
BEFORE YOU
AND FOR THOSE WHO WILL COME
AFTER YOU.
YOU'RE SHOWING THEM
WE'RE ALL CONNECTED
AND NONE OF US
STAND ALONE IN THE UNIVERSE.

Table of Contents

LifeSketch Can be Adapted to Your Needs and Style

You can work independently

Write your own memories and family stories.

You can work with a friend or in a small group

You can take turns interviewing each other and/or sharing stories.

You can work with family

Interview family members and share your stories.

What Can You Create?

Written Stories
To Share with Loved
Ones

Well Labeled Photos that
Tell a Story

Recorded Interviews
In person or virtual

INTRODUCTION

This book is a wish come true. It's the wish of every person who has said "I wish I had asked…"

…why our family left the old country
…where my grandfather served in WWII
…for my mother's favorite recipes
…what daily life was like for my dad growing up on a farm
…what my great-grandparents were like
…why my grandparents divorced
… why I have close DNA matches I don't recognize
…why I am not a DNA match to my maternal grandparents
…if we have relatives who fought in the Revolutionary War
… who can we blame for the family nose

I have been enamored with family history since I was a teenager. I didn't care about the names and dates, but I loved the stories. My grandmother's house dated back to the 1800s. The plastered walls of the entryway had a noticeable patch that sliced from the ceiling to the floor. The family story was that the entryway had been hit by a cannonball during the Civil War. I played under the scarred plaster walls as a child and imagined what that day must have been like for the family that lived there.

When I first started doing family history work professionally, I worked hard to find vital records (birth, marriage, and death records), military service, and census records. Those records are crucial to conducting sound research, but inevitably, I presented them to clients with very mixed results.

Most people found them interesting but records alone rarely create that spark of connection with our grandparents and great-grandparents. Inevitably, my clients would say

at some point, "That's interesting. Boy, I wish I had asked _______________ about
_______________."

What filled in those blanks ranged from the mildly curious (e.g., I wonder why my grandparents got married out of state) to the heartbreaking (e.g., I wonder why my grandfather left his family in such abject poverty).

One friend said to me, "My grandmother was a seamstress for the royal family of Czar Nicholas. When I was a child, I shared a room with my grandmother, and it never occurred to me to ask anything about it!"

The wish that comes true in this book is that "I wish I had asked…" will be said far less often.

My goal with this book is to help you uncover the stories you want to learn from other family members and to motivate you to tell your own stories. This can be a solitary endeavor or one full of social interaction. You decide. You can work with family members, but you also can work with a friend. Friends can interview each other or share written stories.

This process is usually fun and always meaningful.

But my life isn't very interesting!

This is the most common objection I hear and it's also one of the primary reasons our family members are left wishing they had asked more questions. You may feel this way yourself, or the person you want to interview may say this. It helps to be reminded that each person is granted one life with a particular set of experiences and a particular set of character qualities that responds to the events that happen to her.

I asked an older relative what it was like to grow up during the Great Depression. She looked puzzled by my question. "Well, we did what we had to do!" was all she could think to say. Her life experience was her "normal," and she couldn't see anything exceptional about it.

Our individual experiences often don't seem remarkable or worthy of conversation until we realize that each of us has lived a unique life. I was talking with a woman who grew up in a refugee camp for Latvians that was run by Americans on German soil. I was captivated. "I hope you write those stories down!" I gushed. She shook her head in puzzlement, "Oh there was nothing interesting about it. It all seemed very normal to me."

While I often found the stories of older relatives interesting, I was pretty sure that my childhood growing up in the suburbs of Baltimore, Maryland in the 1970s was not compelling material. As happens to all of us, a younger relative (in my case, my daughter) sat gobsmacked one afternoon after she had explored my parents' house and realized the rotary phones attached to the wall allowed someone else to pick up another phone in the house and join or listen to the conversation. I could see her plotting as she side-eyed her older brother. It's a mundane detail of my life, but it doesn't take too many experiences like this before you begin to realize 1) "Wow, I'm old" and 2) my childhood was vastly different from hers in more ways than rotary phones.

Stories that Illuminate

I spent two decades in the publishing industry and found myself relieved to be laid off during the economic downturn of 2008-2010. I still love books. I love reading. What wore me down was the business side of publishing. If you want your staff to get a paycheck, you are forced to buy stories that appeal to the widest possible audience – essentially the lowest common denominator.

Amazing, meaningful books are written and published every year, but if you work in the industry, you are lucky if your company gets to publish two fabulous books in a year. That means you spend most of your time working on the publishing equivalent of clickbait.

What I love about uncovering the real-life drama in family history, is that every story matters. It matters to the people who lived it and to their descendants. We go to the movie theater and pay money to spend a couple of hours swept up in someone else's story without realizing we have amazing, true stories from our own families that affect us much more directly.

Let's face it, all of us probably have an ancestor and a moment in our family story that if things had gone differently… we wouldn't be here. That relative that managed to survive the 1918 Flu Pandemic made it possible for you to be holding this book. Do you have a relative who survived WWII? What did your ancestors do to endure the Great Depression? I love the stories that make us who we are. The stories – once known – connect us to a bigger story that gives us that feeling of curling our toes into the warm soil on a summer day – a sense of roots.

Doing family history research as a hobby and now as a profession has shown me in stark fashion how the world of technology and progress has outpaced our need for roots and connections. The freedom to move frequently and work virtually has left us with an unintended consequence of losing longstanding connections to people and communities. Many of us only need to go back to our parents' or grandparents' generation to see lives rooted in small communities that needed to be interdependent to survive. Multiple generations grew up in the same town and your family history was intricately interwoven into the community's history.

A 2010 study out of Emory University looked at the development of adolescent identity and well-being related to how much kids knew about their family history. The researchers started by asking adolescents 20 yes or no questions to find out if they knew such things as how their parents met, or where they grew up and went to school. What they found was that kids who knew more about their family history were more likely to have a positive sense of self-worth, an ability to plan for the future and fewer problem behaviors.[1]

The researchers suggest that an awareness of the ways parents and grandparents dealt with challenges and opportunities in the past can be beneficial to an adolescent in the present, even if the parent or grandparent made foolish mistakes. It's a form of vicarious learning that gives adolescents more perspective on their own challenges.

While the study was focused particularly on adolescent development, the researchers suggest that a knowledge of family history gives a sense of connection regardless of age.

> *It may, for example, be the case that in family narratives we … have a figurative thread which not only holds families together but contributes to continuity across the life spans of individual members of the families, regardless of their developmental state.[2]*

In other words, we never reach an age where we do not benefit from a sense of family connection.

---

[1] *"Do You Know…" The Power of Family History in Adolescent Identity and Well-Being.* Fiyush, Robin, Marshall, Duke, Bohanek, Jenifer G.. Research supported through a grant from the Alfred P. Sloan Foundation to the Emory Center for Myth and Ritual in American Life. 2010.
[2] ibid

When I decided to self-publish my father's memoir, I was drawn into the details of his young life in the mountains of West Virginia during the Depression. His father (my grandfather) was a tenant farmer who was hired by local orchards to work as a foreman. With each job my grandfather was offered a house, a garden plot, and a dollar a day. Plumbing and electricity, optional.

Here's one of my father's earliest memories:

> *We had a spring house. I only remember seeing inside one time, when [my older sister] dragged me along on an errand. There was the open mouth of the spring at one end. The water flowed out through a prepared channel across the floor on the right side. The channel was just deep enough for gallon crocks to sit in the water. These crocks would hold milk for a day, cream for a week, or butter and cottage cheese for longer. This was the only cool place in the summer and was kept neat and clean.*
>
> *The spring house was strictly off-limits for me when I was alone. My mother's brother had drowned as a young man, and she was adamant that children were to be kept away from water – even the spring house. It didn't help that my older brother George had fallen into a similar spring when he was two.[3]*

Figure 1: My father (left) Glen Whitacre about 1935

My father probably told me this story before, but as everyone who was ever a kid can testify, kids don't always pay attention! And we usually come to regret it. This simple account of a mundane event in my father's life took on new meaning when I read it in his memoir.

First, it explained some things about my grandmother Lottie. She came to take care of me and my sister when my parents traveled to Spain in the 1970s. We lived near a tributary to the Chesapeake Bay and my grandmother would not let me out of the yard the entire time my parents were away. My grandmother was a sweet lady, so I was really confused about

---

[3] Whitacre, C. Glenvil. *Come Back and See Us: A Childhood in Depression-era Virginia. 2019, pp. 18-19.* Available only on Amazon.com.

why I had been "grounded." Now I realize she was afraid I'd drown in the river that was a short distance from my back yard.

Second, my father's first refrigerator was a mountain stream?! Seriously?! I'm sure my father explained a spring house to me as a teenager, but clearly, I must have been daydreaming about my new Barry Manilow album (*Oh, Mandy!*) or wondering whether Barry Gibb would ever know my name. (I had a thing for men named Barry.)

Reading my father's account now that I was a grown woman with a family and a fancy icemaker that perpetually needs repair, the stark simplicity of the life my grandparents led helped me imagine a life very different from the one I live now. Not that I'd want to trade places, but instead that it made me aware that things I deemed *necessities* were not required by earlier generations to live full and interesting lives. The story gave me a new perspective and inadvertently imparted some wisdom.

My mission is to be sure you aren't one of those people who mournfully says, "I wish I had asked my mother/grandmother/brother/sister/father, etc. about that." And if you are one of the elders in your family, I hope you make sure your descendants know as much as you do about where they come from.

Heroes and Villains

Families are complicated. I work at the Ernest Hemingway Birthplace Museum in Oak Park, Illinois. We have thousands of visitors every year who want to learn about Ernest Hemingway's childhood and his extraordinary family.

Ernest Hemingway tends to be a polarizing character. For some, Hemingway evokes only negative images of a drunken, depressed, misogynist. For others, he is appreciated as a groundbreaking, world-class author.

The members of his family were no less colorful. His mother, Grace Hall Hemingway, was a classically trained opera singer who ran her own successful music studio at the turn of the 20th century when most women were expected to recede from the limelight after they were married and had children. She was a suffragette and later became a recognized landscape painter. Hemingway's relationship with his mother became difficult, particularly when he began to spread his own artistic wings. He bluntly told people he hated his mother and he blamed her for the suicide of his father.

After Hemingway's death, photographs of 2- or 3-year-old Ernest wearing a dress and a frilly bonnet came to public attention. For those who were aware of his feelings about his mother, those photographs became proof – Exhibit A – of Grace's contribution to Hemingway's ultimately tortured soul. The heroes and villains in the Hemingway family are a subject of contested debate in literary circles.

In reality, the labels assigned to family members often tell us more about the family or larger society than they do about the individual who has been labeled. One way we can study other ethnic cultures is to notice who are considered the heroes and the villains. In other words, what behaviors and accomplishments are praised and what is condemned. Family culture is no different. Many families have deeply engrained stories of the "bad guys" and the "good guys." Stories get handed down full of condemnation and judgment that may or may not be deserved.

Don't accept those characterizations at face value and don't worry about the characterizations of others. Once you begin recording family stories, it won't be long before you bump up against some opposing interpretations of family history. This is particularly true when there has been a loss in a family – a divorce, a suicide, etc. It's human nature to wonder whom we can blame.

Try not to put yourself in the middle as an arbiter of who is right and who is wrong. See yourself as a reporter or a police officer who is just interested in hearing the "facts" from your witness. The account is still valuable as part of a larger picture.

Stay as nonjudgmental as possible because that stance is most likely to reveal the most information. A judgmental attitude shuts people down. Your goal is to help people feel comfortable talking about things they have no obligation to share with you.

Of course, this can also apply if you are telling your own story. Regret and judgment often cloud our retelling of stories – whether we are judging ourselves or others. When in doubt, think about a memory and ask yourself what you experienced with your five senses. What did you see, hear, taste, smell, etc.? Imagine you have a video camera filming your memory. What would the camera pick up? Then it's perfectly fine to add how you interpreted or judged that experience. It's surprising how often things we think we *know*, we actually don't know for sure.

I requested the divorce records for my grandparents and I was disappointed that all I got back was an index card. It indicated that my grandfather had filed for the divorce and the stated reason was simply listed as "adultery" – presumably by my grandmother. That grandmother died in the 1980s and had suffered several strokes that left her mute for most of my childhood. I didn't have any context with which to process this information. And it potentially meant that the man I thought was my grandfather was not my biological grandfather.

I felt conflicted. Admittedly, part of me wanted to be judgmental. Part of me wondered whether there was important context missing. My mother told me that my grandparents had worked as servants in the house of a well-to-do family in Virginia. My grandmother had married at the age 14 after her mother died. The employer's family had at least one son living on the property and my mother secretly wondered if he was her father.

Before my mother passed away, a simple DNA test showed that my grandfather was her biological father. But the context of knowing my orphaned grandmother was working as a servant in the house that included a wealthy single man raised some possibilities that might be viewed differently today. I am likely to never know the truth about that situation. What was labeled simply as adultery in 1935 may today be labeled as child abuse or rape. Whatever the truth, the spirit of being non-judgmental has the added benefit of being the most intellectually honest.

The LifeSketch process won't answer all your questions, and those who know the answers may or may not be willing or able to talk to you. But just like a police officer or a journalist, you are taking one person's account of events and it might help shed light on the bigger picture – someday.

1

How to Decide What Stories to Capture

I chose the name Life*Sketch* for this process because I want you to feel free to put some marks on a page and see what happens. In the same way, a painter may start with a sketch, you can bring a feeling of play and experimentation to telling your stories. Some sketches are never completed. You may start a story and decide it's going nowhere and abandon it.

If you really want to pique interest in your descendants make sure to leave interesting cliffhangers to your abandoned stories, "I sat quietly waiting and watching the clock. It dawned on me that what happened in the next 10 minutes would probably set the course of my life. When it was finally time, I lifted the pregnancy test off the bathroom counter and…."

I have a file in my desk labeled "writing." I just tuck those abandoned or partial stories in there and move on. At some point, you might want to come back to it. Don't overthink it.

Throughout this book, I will often talk in terms of *writing* your stories. But there are other ways to tell stories. You can audio record or video record stories and interviews. If that sounds complicated to you, just hail the closest young person with a smartphone. It takes very little effort to record these days.
When you've gone through the process of LifeSketch a few times, you will have at least a few short stories about the people and places that are meaningful to you. And LifeSketch is intended to be open-ended. You can come back as often as you like to add to your LifeSketch. If life interrupts, no problem. Come back any time. You can work until you have a full-length biography or family history if you choose. But if all you do is write down a few good stories to share with your grandkids, you have succeeded at LifeSketch.

The publishing industry regularly holds writer conferences. The idea is for publishing professionals to meet new up-and-coming writers. Publishing professionals and successful writers put on workshops during the conference to help new writers develop their craft. Occasionally a writers' conference would lead to a new publishing contract, but usually, we spent a lot of time disappointing writers by telling them their stories weren't saleable.

A dear woman would approach us with – for example – the story she lovingly wrote about her father's service in WWII. She had spent months preparing to come to this conference and in literally 15 minutes we would send her packing with her puddle of crushed dreams.

Here is what I learned: stories do not have to be saleable to be important or meaningful. Storytelling is as old as human speech. It's important. Stories don't have to be saleable to be good. Let go of notions that writing is only important if it's published.

My sister and I were biking near a river the other day and passed this group of ladies sitting in lawn chairs sketching and painting scenic views of the river. I couldn't help the urge to steal a glance at the sketches and then look quickly over my shoulder at what they were painting. My sister lost sight of where she was going and nearly took out a jogger using the same path. It was hard to take our eyes off them! They were relaxed but focused. That's the space I want you to try to find as we get you started making your first LifeSketch.

Exercise #1

Pick any story you want to tell and do it. You can write it, you can audio record it – you can literally sketch it if you are artistically inclined. I'll put some prompts below that you can use if they are helpful. There are additional prompts in the appendix and there are blank pages throughout the book you can use to write. If your story is a paragraph or a few pages, it doesn't matter. Just relax and focus.

Note: You might be tempted to skip the exercises, but I promise you that doing them will teach you more than reading all the best tips in the world.

- What relative did you meet who went the farthest back in your family tree (e.g., great-grandmother, grandfather, etc.)? What happened when you visited them (imagine what could you videotape)? Did your family ever talk about that relative? What were your impressions?

- Tell us about the house or apartment where you grew up. What did you like about it or hate about it? Did you have a favorite place? What was your best memory there? How long did you live there?

- Who was your first best friend? How did you meet? What did you like to do together? Why do you think you became best friends? How did you feel when you were with him/her?

Exercises and Notes
(Relax. You Can't Get It Wrong)

You are the world's best expert on YOU

2

LifeSketch Level One: Context

While I had a career working with writers, I approach LifeSketch more as a family historian than as a writer. Therefore, the process of LifeSketch focuses on getting down the details that will be useful information about your family history.

To help you remember the steps, I use the acronym CARE.

C – Context: Background and Basic Timeline

A – Account: Chose One Story at a Time

R – Reflect: Connect to the Heart

E – Enlarge: Add and Share Stories

Context is the first and the most important step that people need to create when they are telling a story. It provides the **background** and **basic timeline**. When I interview people about their family history, I find myself asking a seemingly endless list of follow-up questions in order to understand what they are trying to tell me. The reason? Family shorthand.

Family shorthand includes all those background details that only your immediate family is likely to know, but others may not. For example, I have done a lot of research on my husband's side of the family. I even put together an extensive LifeSketch of his grandparents. Yet, I found myself at a family reunion listening to his family share memories of "Chick," "Doll" and "Rastus," and I didn't know who they were talking about. No one in my husband's family has those names on their birth certificates. Turns out, "Chick" was a nickname for my husband's grandfather, Charles. Charles's siblings, Jennie and Ralph, were nicknamed Doll and Rastus. At one point I commented that the family liked to use nicknames and an odd quiet settled over the group. Not only had it not occurred to them, even after I said it, someone said, "I don't think that's true!" (What do I know? I'm just an in-law.) Knowing the family shorthand came in handy when I later inherited some letters written by Chick, Doll and Rastus.

Lots of families will also choose special names for their children's grandparents. In my family, my dad's mom was "Granny" while my mom's mom was "Grandma." Some families use names like Nana, Papa, etc. I can't tell you how often clients have pulled out old family pictures only labeled with nicknames or unhelpful labels like "me." This becomes especially challenging when pictures are shared with nieces, nephews or cousins.

Let's look at this same problem in a written LifeSketch:

Figure 2: Use full names when labeling pictures. "Me" won't be helpful to future generations

I don't know the time frame, but my mother's father had died leaving my mother's mother with four children and no means of support. My father's father agreed to marry her with the condition that she find some other place for her children.

Besides being a rather odd family arrangement, it's also rather difficult to follow. Try this:

My father's parents were Josh and Sarah Whitacre. My mom's parents were George and Laura DeHaven. Sarah Whitacre and George DeHaven died about the same time, and their spouses decided to get married, though Laura was required to find some other place for her children before she married Josh.

Even my suggested changes assume that the writer has introduced himself and his immediate family, but you get the idea.

There are two ways you can create context for your stories. If you are not an experienced writer, it's okay to create an answer key or cheat sheet that gets attached to the front of your story. Simply make a list of the characters and as much info as you know about each – almost like you are reading the cast listing in a playbill.

This story is written/told by [who] me, Glen Whitacre.
It takes place in [where] Glengary, West Virginia.
It takes place around [when] 1906
"Mother" is Lottie Catherine DeHaven (born 1898)
"Father" is Holmes Love Whitacre

"Josh" is Caleb Joshua Whitacre, Holmes's father [who]

The more detail you put in your list, the better. If you know any dates such as birth or death dates, include them. Some families have multiple generations with the same name. I worked with a family that was descended from four generations of men with the first name William, so we usually had to include a birth year to distinguish them, such as "William (b. 1875) lived in Sweden until….."

The other way to create context is to carefully weave it into your story. At some point each new character should get a full name and some background info. This is less confusing for the reader but will require some additional effort on your part. To help you remember what you need to include, make a checklist you can consult while you are writing.

WHO – list all your characters and <u>how they are related to the main character</u> in your story

WHERE – where does the story take place – town, state/province (and country if the family lived in more than one country)

WHEN – add dates, even if they are approximate. If you don't know a date relate it to something else known in the timeline like "Before Paul got married…"

OTHER HELPFUL BACKGROUND – what should the reader know about that place and time (i.e., Virginia during the Great Depression). Is there other background information the reader will need to appreciate this story? For example, if you want to tell a story about a coal mining accident, you may need to explain a little about the process of coal mining for readers to understand what happened.

We are basically covering all the things a journalist would ask: Who, what, when, where, and, possibly, why. I know it seems basic, but can you imagine a news article that did not include these items?

Breaking News

*Somebody's uncle was arrested in a town at some point. Not sure what
he was arrested for but somebody's aunt must be very angry because he
was seen sleeping on the porch.*

The lack of detailed information can make stories confusing and obscure the elements that make stories compelling.

Good Background Questions

Once you've decided whether you want to do a sketch about yourself or someone else, start by answering as many of the questions listed in Exercise #2 as you can. If you don't remember or can't get an answer from your interviewee, go to the next question.

The goal is to create a basic timeline. Once you've done a timeline, you'll have a better idea of what stories you want to tell. You don't want to spend too much time on minutiae only to realize your interviewee is a decorated war veteran and you didn't prepare any questions on that topic.

I also want to emphasize that this exercise is intended to be the first step in creating a LifeSketch, but it may end up being the only step. My friend Diana works with hospice patients to help them record stories about their life. This raises the possibility that the person you are interviewing may not be capable of providing more than step one. Whatever information you get is a gift to future generations.

Older folks with memory issues should not be left off your list of potential interviewees. Keep in mind many older folks have trouble with their short-term memory but can often recount every detail about their childhood. After I finished my father's memoir, I got an email from a man whose mother had been classmates with my father. He said his mother had memory loss, but when he read my father's accounts of high school, she remembered something about every person mentioned. Don't assume just because someone has memory issues that it's not worth interviewing them.

It's also common for people with memory issues to have good days and bad days. So, you need to go into those interviews with a spirit of flexibility and good humor. My mother suffered with dementia and there were times I'd want to ask her about a specific time in her life like elementary school and she would launch into a story about when she met my father. No worries! Go with the flow! If you show up with anxiety or rigid goals, you are more likely to shut your subject down.

Work with a Partner

One final note before we begin our next exercise. If you intend to write your own
LifeSketch, you do not have to work alone. It can be a lot of fun to do LifeSketch with a
partner. You can take turns interviewing each other and writing down the answers.
Sometimes talking to someone else can give you better results. Your interviewer is more
likely to ask clarifying questions. It can be a lot fun to sit down with a good friend, your
beverage of choice and share this exercise. You can even work with someone over the phone
or on a video call.

Exercise #2: Creating a Basic Timeline

If you run out of space for any of your answers, use blank pages at the back of the book.

Where and when were you born? What name is on your birth certificate?

Where did you live while growing up?

Who lived at home with you when you were young?

How far did you go in school? Did you like school?

What were your favorite pastimes as a kid?

Did you have a favorite relative growing up? Why?

What did you do after you finished your schooling?

Where did you live as an adult?

What jobs did you have?

Did you marry? Where did you meet?

Did you have children? How many? What are their names and birthdates?

Did you serve with any organizations like the military, Peace Corps, Doctors Without Borders, etc.?

What are you most proud of?

What do you want people to remember about you?

How would your friends describe you?

Anything else you want to tell me about your life?

If you're tempted to think these questions are too basic, you will be surprised how many people don't know the maiden names of their grandmothers or how many children they had. If this is as far as you plan to go in your LifeSketch, skip to Chapter 5 about how to "Enlarge" your LifeSketch.

3

LifeSketch Level Two: Account

C – Context: Background and Basic Timeline
A – Account: Choose One Story at a Time
R – Reflect: Connect to the Heart
E – Enlarge: Add and Share Stories

If you've managed to capture the big picture facts of someone's life or your own, fabulous! You've already created a keepsake. If you're ready to do more, let's pick a specific story and elaborate.

Doing the last exercise creates the context and background for smaller stories, or accounts, that you can begin to tell. The metaphor for this entire process is sketching. You're not trying to tell the story of your entire life. At least not today. We are creating a series of sketches.

In this step, you pick one story to tell and tell it. This is important because one of the primary reasons clients tell me they stop collecting stories is that they get overwhelmed. The project feels too big. They find themselves feeling stuck. They try to go chronologically and get weighted down in some part of their story that is boring or unpleasant and they stop.

Writer Anne Lamott has a wonderful book about her craft titled *Bird by Bird*. She chose the title from one of her early experiences writing a school report about the birds of North America. She felt overwhelmed. Her mom's advice? Just go bird by bird. Small steps, and an attitude of play and experimentation are far more likely to help you reach your goal.

You do not need to tell stories in chronological order. Follow the story that is top of mind and closest to your heart. One of the ways I choose stories to write is by paying attention to where my mind goes when I'm doing dishes or driving. Chances are that the places your mind wanders are often the places your heart really wants to explore.

I have had clients that find doing stories out of order to be very disconcerting. One way you can address this is to make a list/timeline of the key stories you want to tell. You can check them off in any order and put them in chronological order later.

The important thing is to include stories that connect to your heart. Because this is a family history exercise and not just a writing class, we do want real facts – names, places, etc. – but let's put those people and places in the events that are meaningful for you. That will show your descendants not just names and dates but something about your character and help them understand what it's like to be you.

Stories About What You Love

Stories about what you love can be some of the most intimate stories you can share. Best-selling author Joyce Maynard encourages her writing students to make a list of things they obsess about.[4] Joyce identifies some of her own obsessions that include defining events in her life – such as the death of her mother – as well as innocuous obsessions like cowboy boots, figure skating and Dolly Parton. Obsessions can tell people a lot about you <u>if you are careful to unpack the meaning</u> behind your obsessions and not just facts about your areas of interest.

I am not a baseball fan. I have attended exactly one professional baseball game and every time the batter connected with the ball, I was looking somewhere else. Yet, one of my favorite books is *The Chosen* by Chaim Potok in which one baseball game is the focus of the first half of the book. Potok pulls me into the story by infusing the baseball game with the meaning the game has for the characters. I've heard adult men tell stories that brought

> **Pro Tip:** Make a list of things you obsess about, like baseball, cooking, or social justice. Write a story about one of your obsessions. To keep it interesting to your reader, don't just relay facts about your area of interest, tell people why it's meaningful to you. Why is baking bread such a fulfilling hobby for you? What does it remind you of? What situations have you personally experienced that connect you with social justice? Etc.

---

[4] Maynard, Joyce. *Writing Your Stories.* Video course available on thegreatcourses.com.

them to tears about going to baseball games with their father or favorite uncle. I don't just want you to tell me baseball stats, tell me why baseball is so meaningful for you.

I like to knit. I am a mediocre knitter. I have a terrible time making sweaters and things that are actually supposed to fit people. Scarves are what you knit when you can't properly size things. I have enough scarves to cover the Statue of Liberty head to toe. Do I need that many scarves? No. If I want to write about my obsession with knitting scarves, I need to tell you what makes it meaningful to me.

Knitting makes me feel connected to my grandmother who survived the Depression making quilts out of old clothes and flour sacks. She embroidered plain white pillowcases because she could make something look fancy with just a needle and some thread. When I take a ball of yarn and make something useful or beautiful, it has a spiritual quality for me. I can be a creator, not just a consumer.

Life Defining Events: Traumas and Secrets

Often, we have one thing or a few things that we consider defining events in our life. These can be meaningful, but difficult things to write about. When I was six years old my college-aged brother died by suicide. It was such a life-altering blow to our family that I internalized it as part of my identity. I was "the girl whose brother committed suicide." Anytime we identify deeply with a life event it is fertile soil to use as a subject for a LifeSketch.

A "life defining event" might also be a good thing – a contest you won, a special trip you took, etc. Wherever there is meaning for you, you have the basis for an important story. In the wake of my brother's suicide, a kind neighbor helped me enter a flower arranging contest and I won honorable mention. I reveled in my neighbor's one-on-one attention and in the ability to create something beautiful when the rest of my life was ugly.

Good life-defining events are usually easier to write about, but I want to give special attention to the traumatic events and family secrets.

Families have their own rules, often unspoken, but no less binding. Many times, those rules involve what we are and are not allowed to talk to about. In my home, we did not openly express feelings except for frustration or anger. My father was a wiz at fixing things around the house, but if projects started to go sideways, we all ran for our bedrooms to hide. Not that he was ever violent, but there was no talking to him when he was frustrated and we didn't know enough to be helpful. My mom would often feel hurt by my father, but hurt feelings weren't allowed so her feelings came out as anger too. You can imagine the tinder box in my house when my brother died. We all had lots of feelings and only one feeling – anger – was allowed to be expressed.

By the time I went away to college, I had developed a very stoic facade. I still remember getting into an argument with my college roommate and at one point she said, exasperated, "Don't you feel anything?" In truth, I was feeling A LOT but I had no practice at sharing what I was feeling.

The rules in your house may have been very different, but if you find yourself questioning whether you are *allowed* to tell a story, it's a good possibility that you've bumped into one of the family rules.

Writing this section of the book before my parents died would have been difficult for me. My parents were flawed, but I love them fiercely and I would never want to appear ungrateful for the sacrifices they made to raise me. Telling some of the hard stories requires allowing two truths to coexist: the truth that family members may have caused a great amount of pain and the truth that we still deeply love them. You don't have to choose between those two realities. Think of them like two peas in the same pod.

I have a dear friend who experienced this dynamic in the extreme. Her brother murdered a child. We speculate now that he may have been schizophrenic, but he wasn't diagnosed at the time. The family had to abandon the life that they knew and move out of state to have any hope of a normal life. My friend was a child when the family moved, but she was given strict instructions not to talk about the situation in their new neighborhood so as not to draw a media frenzy to their new hometown. In most cases we are  not told so directly about what we are allowed to share, but we still know the family rules.

Many families that have dealt with addiction, abuse or mental illness have learned to keep secrets, sometimes for good reason. Many of these challenges can be met with judgment instead of support.

GIVE YOURSELF PERMISSION TO TELL YOUR STORY. If it helps to hear someone else say it: I hereby give you permission to tell your story! You don't actually need my permission, of course, but I want to give you something to say to yourself when you're tempted to think. "Oh no. I can't tell that story."

I also want to emphasize that telling your story is one decision you can make. Another decision we will also cover in a later chapter is the decision about who gets to read your story. Just because you tell it doesn't mean you want it printed on the front page of the newspaper or in a social media post. You get to decide whom you tell, and you don't have to decide that before you write the story.

I want to make an important comment to those of you who have suffered severe trauma or abuse. It is NOT always a good idea to sit by yourself and relive something traumatic. You may need the support of a friend or therapist. If you begin to feel completely overwhelmed by your story, it's a good sign that you need to put it down and seek support. Once you've had an opportunity to share that weight, you can always come back to writing your story.

You likely know the areas of your life that are difficult to talk about but what if you are interviewing someone who has experienced trauma? I have a friend whose father served in WWII and was part of the amphibious landing on D-Day. He was never able to discuss his experience with his son. As much as we all admired my friend's father and wanted to hear his story, it was his story.

Your interviewee always gets to be in the driver's seat when it comes to what stories they share. It is not wise or respectful to push someone to tell a story they are not ready to share. You may retraumatize them by pressuring them to talk if they can still feel overwhelmed when discussing their experience.

If you are interviewing someone about their war experiences, you can anticipate the likelihood that you should tread lightly. Sometimes, though, you might stumble upon trauma in an unexpected place – which, let's face it, trauma can be a part of any seemingly mundane topic you ask about.

I never had the opportunity to meet my husband's grandmother. By all accounts she was a character! She was a single mother for many years and was tough as nails. She started and ran a successful coal business during the Great Depression. She donated a great deal of money to build one of the community churches, which then turned around and kicked her out when she opened a restaurant that served (gasp!) liquor.

In doing family research, I requested the court documents from her divorce from her first husband. I was surprised to find testimony that described physical abuse she suffered at the hands of her first husband. As far as I know, she never talked about it. Clearly, that was not a story she was ready to tell during her lifetime.

Use Story Prompts or Special Photographs

When I first started working in publishing, one of my jobs was to write the copy that goes on the back cover of books. The worst part was sitting down to start. A blank sheet of paper that is not supposed to be blank can be very intimidating! If you find yourself feeling stuck when you sit down to write some memories, there are a few tricks that can help you get writing. I often would look at the front cover or reread parts of the book to get ideas.

You can do the same type of things to help you get started. Do you have a few favorite photographs? They are probably your favorite because they remind you of someone or some event that is important to you. Those can be great prompts for stories.

Written prompts or questions can also serve as inspiration. There are plenty of printed and online resources that give you prompts you can use as a springboard for a story. I have included some I like in the appendix of this book.

Pro Tip: Cursive handwriting is no longer taught in most schools so young people can't read it. If you decide to handwrite your stories in cursive, see if you can get a friend or relative to type them up so they will be more easily accessible to future generations.

Summary: Guidelines for Choosing a LifeSketch Story

1. You do not need to tell the stories of your life chronologically.

2. Tell stories that connect to your passions, obsessions or defining life events – stories that connect to your heart.

3. Remember to create a cheat sheet for all the contextual details of your story (who, what, when, and where) If possible, include them in the body of the story. If not, list them as a preface to your story.

4. If you are not sure where to start, use a story prompt or question and **just start!** Once you start writing, you often find yourself writing about the story they wanted to tell but didn't know it!

Exercise #3 Write a LifeSketch

Let's do it!

1. **Pick your medium**

Will you write long-hand? At a computer? Audio or video record? What would you like the final "product" to be?

2. **Select a story**

Remember, the stakes are LOW. If you pick something you end up not liking, you can choose something else next time. Don't overthink it.

You can use one of the story prompts listed at the back of the book or choose from one listed below. Looking back at your answers from Exercise #2 might also spark an idea for a story. You can write on the blank pages provided in this book if you'd like.

- In the summer when you weren't in school, what was a day like for you? What did you love doing? Is there anything you hated doing? Did you have chores? What were they?

- What was the biggest obstacle you had to overcome in childhood? How did it affect you as an adult?

- Did you have important religious or cultural traditions during your childhood? What were they and how did you feel about them?

3. **Don't Let Discomfort and Doubt Silence You**

Most of us feel discomfort at starting a new project. If you're like me, you will begin to have doubts the minute you sit down to do it. I feel that all the time, and I've worked with enough professional writers to assure you even they often struggle with starting projects. When I sat down to write this book, I had a barrage of negative thoughts pop up in my head. *What if my book is terrible? What if I don't have anything helpful to share?* For a lot of us, that is to be expected. I've gotten to the point where I often have to answer these questions in my head: *What if you try something and it fails? OH WELL! Won't know until you try!*

      If all else fails, set a timer for 20 or 30 minutes and just start writing. It doesn't even need to make sense, just the act of writing will likely help "unfreeze" you.

ProTip: If you find yourself getting bogged down or not finishing stories, ask yourself if you can make the story smaller. Making the scope of the project too big is the primary reason clients get discouraged and stop working. LifeSketch is modular; you can tell one part of the story at a time.

Exercises and Notes
(Relax. You Can't Get It Wrong)

Dear Past, Thank You

for the People Who Made My Life Better....

4

LifeSketch Level Three: Reflect

C – Context: Background and Basic Timeline
A – Account: Choose One Story at a Time
R – Reflect: Connect to the Heart
E – Enlarge: Add and Share Stories

In the movie, *Groundhog Day* weatherman Phil Connors (Bill Murray) finds himself in a time loop reliving the same day over and over again. Phil eventually figures out that the different choices he makes during his day have different results. Phil begins to learn from his mistakes.

After the movie was released, a wide variety of fascinating interpretations of the movie began to circulate. Religious groups of different persuasions saw metaphors for rebirth and purgatory. Others suggested it was a metaphor for psychoanalysis, military boredom, and even economic theory.

Meaning is highly subjective and we often assume what we derive from a story or an experience is obvious to everyone. Sometimes the meaning of an experience is so touching, we have difficulty putting it into words. It's important when you are writing a LifeSketch that you make it clear why a story is meaningful to you. Tell the reader why it connects to your heart.

Consider this section of a LifeSketch:

When I was about five or six years old, I was outside looking for something to do. That's what kids did in the 70's. Kids TV

This story provides some context and gives an account of what happened. What it doesn't tell us is what this childhood story meant for the writer. Was this a harmless childhood prank or the prelude to something more significant – child abuse, an eating disorder, a lasting friendship with Mrs. Drumm. Maybe it was intended to show free range parenting of the 1970s. "Send them outside until the streetlights come on" seemed to be the one instruction parents were given when they took their kids home from the hospital then.

Most of the time, stories come back to us because they were significant or connect to something significant – like your relationship with a parent or an experience that taught you something about life. At the most basic level, they usually connect to either joy/pleasure or pain/anger.

The story above is mine, and you may be relieved to know that my connections with this story are happy ones. First, I still remember that the strawberry candy tasted scrumptious on a hot, sweaty summer day. Second, when my mom returned from her walk with Mrs. Drumm, she just looked at me and said, "Don't do that again." I was pretty obsessed with being well-behaved since my brother died and the family was in such turmoil. Stealing candy was a fairly rare infraction and it was helpful for me to see that even if I wasn't perfectly behaved, I wasn't going to break my fragile family.

Writing down experiences that happen to us as children can sometimes create unexpected emotions – happy or sad – when we reflect on them as adults. When those experiences happened to us the first time, we only had a childlike worldview and a childlike understanding of events. Once we reflect on them as adults, we now bring our adult perspective which can be radically different. That's part of what can make this process so meaningful. Though, if you suddenly find something feels overwhelming, put down what you are writing.

Now that I am a parent myself, I appreciate so many things I did not appreciate as a kid because they were outside of my experience. Just the act of keeping a roof over our heads now seems like a heroic accomplishment. Even if our family members did not act heroically – perhaps they were anything but heroic – we often gain perspective that brings a sense of compassion to choices they made to try to fix their lives.

Go back and look at one of your stories. Did you communicate how the events in the story made you feel or the effect those events had on you later in life?

Once you've reviewed a story to ensure you've added enough context and told us what the story means to you, you are ready to add some final touches before you share it. One of the most important additions you can make to your story is visual aids.

Add Pictures

Pictures have power. They can clarify, inform and pique interest in our readers. We often get absorbed in our writing and forget about that box of old photos we have stashed away. Make the effort to incorporate your old family photographs into your stories. It adds interest and it also lessens the chance that those photos will end up in a garage sale because no one can identify who is in them. They can also be attractive bait when you are trying to get younger generations interested in your stories. The ability to gaze into the eyes of your great-grandmother in a photograph can be an awe-inspiring experience and will often draw readers into your story.

If you don't have photos, reach out to extended family members. I recently worked with a woman who had roots in Ukraine. We were able to gather interesting stories about the family patriarch Jacob Gerstenfeld, but unfortunately, we did not have any photos of him. I emailed and called members of the extended family but no one was aware that any photographs existed. A few days later, I got the most wonderful email from a cousin explaining that while the family did not have photographs, there was a portrait!

Figure 1: A portrait of Jacob Gerstenfeld helped us connect with Jacob's story.

Jacob Gerstenfeld's story moved me deeply. Many of his children immigrated to America prior to WWII, but because Jacob was Jewish, he was forced by the Nazis to flee to Siberia with one of his children. They battled starvation and brutal mistreatment to survive the war. Being able to connect these stories with the likeness of the man who endured them was a powerful experience for me and for his family.

In addition to photographs of people, there are many other types of visual aids you can consider adding to your project. You could show photos of objects or locations, such as the type of WWII bomber your relative flew, or a picture of the church where your grandparents were married. Maps can also be helpful visuals for some stories. Images of newspaper headlines can grab a readers' attention. Add a picture or an early magazine advertisement of the type of car the family drove.

Ideally, you want to intersperse photos throughout your stories. If you are comfortable with basic word processing software, there are ways to include photographs within your text. I am writing this in Microsoft Word, which allows me to insert photos and illustrations. Inserting photos is the best way to bring the visual aids close to the relevant text. You can do a quick internet search for directions on how to insert photographs in whatever word processing software you use.

If you are not proficient with word processing software, you can insert copies of photos on separate pages. For example, include your favorite picture of your mother alongside a story you write about her. You could also make a scrapbook that includes your stories and your photographs. You can learn more about caring for precious family photos in chapter 10.

Have Someone You Trust Review Your Work

If you are ready to share your LifeSketch with friends and family, start small and have someone you trust read it over and give you feedback. Be clear about what kind of feedback you want. Do you want them to point out missing words and correct punctuation? Do you want them to give you feedback about how you structured your story? If you feel you are finished with the story, feedback about how to rewrite it is not going to feel good.

One of the most important things I encourage you to request is that your readers check for clarity. Can they follow the people, relationships and places in your story? If something confuses them, it will likely confuse others.

Another benefit to having someone you trust read stories before you share them broadly is that they can help flag anything that might upset people in the family unintentionally. This is especially important if you are talking about complicated or delicate family situations. My family tree has two step siblings who got married. I accidently referred to them as half siblings in a LifeSketch. Fortunately, my trusted reader flagged the mistake.

The more you write, the less intimidating the process will be for you. I worked with a colleague in publishing who later became a fiction author. He told me he had a plan for becoming a published author: write a million words just to practice the act of writing. He'd go home after work and retreat to his office and just push himself to write, write, write. He got his first book published well before he reached a million words, but that exercise helped move him forward. The muscle and emotional memory of just sitting down to write begins to create a virtuous cycle and you will either truly *want* to write or at least won't be as intimidated by a blank page.

> **ProTip:** Ernest Hemingway always made a point to stop writing when he still had something to say. So, if you finish your writing time and you know what you intend to write about next, make yourself a note. It will save you time and help keep the sense of momentum when you sit down to write next time.

Exercise #4 Reflection

1. Go back to the story you wrote in the last exercise. Add a paragraph or two about how you connect to the story. Consider questions like:

- How did the events in your story make you feel?
- Does anything about your story make you feel proud, ashamed, loved, unloved, etc.?
- How did those events affect who you are today?
- What would you like others to know having experienced those events? Do you have any words of wisdom?

2. Consider what visual aids you might want to include with your story.

3. Who can you trust to give you feedback on your story?

Exercises and Notes

(Only you can tell YOUR stories)

You're Wiser than You've Ever Been

5

LifeSketch Level Four: Enlarge

C – Context: Background and Basic Timeline
A – Account: Choose One Story at a Time
R – Reflect: Connect to the Heart
E – Enlarge: Add and Share Stories

Enlarge by Addition

There are several ways you can enlarge your LifeSketch. One way is to keep adding to your story. Framing family history and storytelling as a sketch allows you to break down the lofty goal of finding or communicating family stories into a series of small, manageable projects. The process is intended to be modular – allowing you to come back and do new sketches any time. You can think of it like adding to your artist's portfolio.

At some point, you can enlarge your LifeSketch by deciding to weave your stories together in one coherent book. For now, just focus on expanding your portfolio of family stories.

Enlarge the Audience by Preserving Your Stories

Another way we enlarge our family story projects is to make sure your work is findable by family members – particularly family members who are likely to be stewards of the stories.

Every now and then I go into an antique or resale shop and find a box of old black and white photos from the late 1800s or early 1900s. Inevitably I'll find myself staring into the eyes of a man or woman in a photograph wishing I could ask, "What's your story?"

By the time family pictures end up in a box for sale, the family history is lost. If you're reading this book, you are probably among those who could not imagine old photos of your great-grandparents getting sold to strangers for $1 each. You need to know that it happens all the time. And it's important to understand *why* it happens.

Death is the ultimate boogie man. We avoid thinking about it. We get stressed when we imagine death for ourselves or a loved one. We often ease our distress by imagining unrealistic happy endings where everyone dies peacefully in their sleep, their belongings are handled exactly as they hoped, and there are no hurt feelings among family members about how everything was distributed.

Most of you will know a situation or two that did not end this way. I often have to comfort clients whose family members thoughtlessly disposed of a family heirloom or photos. Even if the loss happened decades ago, the amount of emotion that comes to the surface when they talk about it can be palpable.

One of the challenges in addressing this issue is that there is an infinite number of variables that come into play when someone dies. Who is available to clean out their belongings? Are they being pressured to do things quickly because the house is being sold? Is the person doing the sorting in deep emotional distress? Is there infighting among family members? Is a lawyer involved? Is there a will and – crucially – does the will address items that are digitally stored or saved on the computer?

A new issue in estate planning now is determining who is allowed access to an individual's digital property. Before gay marriage was legalized, I heard a heart-wrenching story of a gay couple where one partner died. They were raising a son together and all the photos were handled by the partner that died. The remaining partner was denied access to the digital account that stored his son's baby pictures. The couple had shared password information before, but – as often happens – the password was reset at some point.

The emphasis on individual privacy laws now can create barriers to family members accessing photos or documents even if the owner clearly would have wanted them to be shared. While making sure your family members have passwords is a great goal, we all know how often we are forced to change passwords either because we have forgotten a password, or the company storing our information requires us to create a new password periodically.

When I was a young supervisor, a wise mentor gave me advice about analyzing work problems. He said, "Ask yourself 'Is this a situation to be managed, or a problem to be solved?'" Some problems never go away and are intrinsic to your line of work – like grouchy customers or bad weather for an outdoor photo shoot. You can't solve that once and for all, but you can come up with contingency plans to manage the problem when it happens. Preserving your family stories is like that. You can't envision every possible problem, – like changes in technology, or a computer crash – but you can do your best to create contingency plans.

I once worked at an archive that held the papers of seven British authors including J.R.R. Tolkien and C.S. Lewis. The wonderful archivist there shared with me what she called "The Backup Rule of Three." This is a strategy used to ensure the important documents and photos in their collection are not lost forever in case of fire, flood or technical failure. In a nutshell, you want to remember 3-2-1 when it comes to important documents and photographs: 3 copies, 2 mediums, 1 offsite.

There are several ways to meet these criteria. So, here's how the Backup Rule of Three applies to a project where I am saving the letters my grandmother wrote to my father. I have the original letters (copy 1), a photocopy of the original (copy 2), and a digital scan on my computer (copy 3). I have used two different mediums because I have paper copies and digital copies. In order to keep one copy in a different location (in case of flood or fire), I subscribe to a service that backs up my computer to another computer miles away.

There are lots of different configurations you can try – none of them can guarantee your material won't be lost, but you are doing everything you can to increase the odds that it will survive.

When my husband was a child, his family's basement flooded and most of his childhood pictures – stored in cardboard boxes – were ruined. We only have a handful of childhood pictures of him now. So, when my kids were little (back when we used to print photos) I would often get double prints and send one set to my sister – who fortunately for me was a very doting aunt who willingly cared for them. She became my offsite storage.

When I began taking digital photographs with my camera, I would print a copy of my photos, upload them to my computer and keep the used memory cards at my office across town. Now that we are in the world of smartphone photos, our family memories are increasingly vulnerable. Photos are rarely printed or even uploaded to our computers. A client recently told me she took photos of her daughter on a phone app – she couldn't remember the name – and she was "pretty sure they are up in the cloud." What if the company that created the app ceases to exist?

Technology is constantly changing, but for right now, you need to be aware that syncing services that are created by Google, Apple, and Microsoft are intended to make your documents available from multiple devices and multiple locations. They are not designed to be long-term storage and their ability to sync with other devices sometimes creates scenarios where you (or someone you gave sharing permission to) may delete a file from your cloud syncing service and unintentionally also delete it from your phone and every other device connected to that account.

What you need is to back up – not sync – your files. You can do this by saving files on a separate hard drive or subscribing to a backup service that automatically backs up your files and holds them on one of their servers for a set period of time. When my laptop crashed last year, I was able to log into my backup service and download files that had been on the computer before it crashed.

If the last couple of paragraphs make no sense to you – don't worry about it! Just do not consider your digital files "somewhere in the cloud" to be your primary copy. Assume it could be gone tomorrow, and make sure you have other ways to store copies.

Enlarge by Sharing Your Stories with Friends and Family

Once you have some stories prepared, what is the best way and the best time to share them with family and friends? Those answers will be different for everyone, but I'll share some tips from my own experience and the experiences of some of my clients.

Holiday Gifts
There is nothing more personal and thoughtful than the gift of family stories. You can print them yourself and put them in a report cover or a three-ring  binder. Holidays are times when people have set aside time and they are focused on family. Don't forget to include copies of old family pictures.

You can also ask someone to video record you telling or reading stories and give the recording as a gift.

Shared Digital Drive

It's possible to have a location online where you can grant access to files and pictures. I have scanned dozens of family photos and family letters. Instead of trying to give everyone in the family their own copy, I created a place online where I store these pictures and stories and I sent invitations to everyone in the family to come and copy what they wanted off of the drive. You'll need someone who is tech-savvy to set it up and manage the digital permissions. One of the upsides of this arrangement is that other people can upload their family pictures to the same location.

Family Reunions

If you are one of the few families that still manages to have family reunions, share your stories at the reunion. People have already set aside time and they are focused on family. You might hand out printed copies early in your time together so people have time to read and ask questions. You could read one of your stories to the group. If that makes you feel nervous, have someone take a cell phone video of you reading the story and show it at the gathering.

At one of my husband's family reunions, we handed out printed copies of a LifeSketch I prepared and then my husband put together a trivia game night with questions about family history. We had teams and gave out prizes. It was a lot of fun.

Side note: I have a lot of trouble getting people – especially women – to agree to have themselves videotaped. I get it. I don't love it either. We all have things about our appearance that we find …. shall I say …. disappointing? I will say this with as much love as I can: GET OVER IT. If you think about a beloved aunt or grandparent you wish you had on videotape, you are not judging her wrinkles and bulges. Just having their essence on video can be such a treasure. In other words, you are not doing it for yourself, but for those who love you. The other nice thing about video recording is you can always delete and start over with your recording. Remember, young people video record themselves constantly for social media apps. Video recording used to be expensive and every take cost money to process film. It's essentially free now, so it doesn't need to look professional. The stakes are LOW.

Self-Publish

If your stories are long enough to benefit from binding, you can also take either printed copies or a digital copy to your local office supply store and they can add a tape or spiral binding.

If you have a longer work, you can actually publish it directly through services like Kindle Direct Print (Amazon.com) or LuLu.com. My husband has a large extended family so when I wrote a family history for his side of the family, I self-published it through Amazon and they were able to order copies off of the Amazon website. This saved me hauling copies to the reunion and paying up front for copies I couldn't be sure I would get paid back for. In order to do this yourself, you need to be proficient at using word processing software. There are also freelancers and companies that will help you get it ready for printing.

Figure 2: A friend self-published his family history and made it available to family on Amazon.com.

If you decide to self-publish you may want to have an editor review your work. There are several websites where you can hire someone to edit your piece for a reasonable price. The range of skill and experience can range widely, as can the fees that are charged. Some editors you find online are English majors in college doing a side hustle. Some will be accomplished editors with many years of experience. I encourage you to start by giving your potential editor a single chapter at an agreed upon price. Get that back and see how you feel about the changes before you give them a large project or more money.

Enlarge by Sharing with Local History and Genealogical Societies

Stories always happen some*where*. Sometimes the value in the story is not only what we learn about the people, but what we learn about the places. I inherited a box of letters written by my husband's beloved grandfather. Charles Cyrus (nicknamed Chick) was born in 1899 in Johnson County, Texas. He grew up in the small town of Cleburne and remembers the first roads that were paved and the first cars that showed up on their streets. He even wrote about the first airplane that landed in Cleburne.

> *Just west of where the Adventist Church now is… there was the gate to the milk cow pasture. The boys brought the family milk cows for pasture during the daytime. The pasture was large, extending about to the county road south of the elementary school and up the hill west of McAnear Creek. (The school is very recent, but the road was roughed out then.) The boys often hiked down in the pasture.*
>
> *Three of us were down there and we heard an airplane. Here it comes. It was a biplane with the pilot sitting in the open. He landed nearby in the cow pasture. We ran over to see the airplane. He had run out of gas.*
>
> *"Will you boys keep the milk cows off my plane while I go get some gas?"*
>
> *We would. When he returned, he gave directions to help him get up again. We held the end of the wings back until he got the engine revved up; then we stepped back and up he went. For watching the plane, he gave us a nickel. We went to the nearest grocery store and got a nickel's worth of peppermint stick candy at 20 cents a pound. We divided and each got 3 1/3 sticks.* [5]

That little anecdote has so many wonderful details about Cleburne in the early 1900s! I contacted the Johnson County Historical Society and the Johnson County Genealogical Society and both organizations were interested in scanned copies of his letters.

When my father wrote about his early life, he – by default – shed light on tenant farmers in West Virginia during the Depression. You may wonder: *Who would be interested in tenant farmers in West Virginia during the Depression?* Historians, sociologists, and genealogists to name a few. I sat next to a woman at a speaker's bureau luncheon, and one of the talks she gave to genealogy and history groups was – you guessed it – on tenant farming.

---

[5] Mayer, Carla Whitacre. *Texas Roots: The Family of Charles and Vivian Cyrus.* Self published and available on Amazon.com. 2018.

I worked with a client whose father, Lt. Bill Wilson, was a WWII bomber pilot. One day, I was helping the family go through his old service records and we found an envelope that simply read "For My Kids." I held up the envelope to see if anyone recognized it, but their expressions were blank.

I carefully opened the envelope and found a letter. "We took off from our bomber base on December 3, 1944, and the target was Berlin," he began simply. As I read the letter aloud, we found a harrowing account of a bomber mission where his plane lost two engines and became separated from the rest of the squadron. They and another bomber limped out of German airspace in an attempt to make it back to England. The other plane went down in the ocean. Because he flew the most direct route to the base, he landed before the rest of the squadron and promptly fell exhausted into his bunk. He woke up to his buddies talking about how much they were going to miss him. Imagine their surprise when he sat up in his bunk!

This is a great story for the family, but it also creates a vivid portrait for anyone who wants to understand what it was like to be a bomber pilot stationed in England in 1944.

Keep in mind that family history is history. There has never been a historical figure who didn't have a family of origin. Personal stories are what make history vibrant and relatable. So, consider sharing stories with organizations that are interested in the details of your stories. You can do a quick internet search by location – such as county and state historical or genealogical societies – or by a historical event – such as The Depression or WWII. Send them a letter or email and see if they are interested.

Keep in mind a lot of organizations have limited space, and may not take physical copies, but many would love digital scans for their collection.

What All Writers Have in Common

Sharing your stories is an act of bravery. I asked a friend who had published several books how she felt when she turned in her most recent manuscript to her publisher. "Naked," she said. "I poured my heart out and it is out there for the world to see."

I've worked with beginning writers and professional writers and you know what they all have in common? Their finished work feels like one of their children. When an author hands you a book, you may just see a book, but to them it is the baby they labored to bring into the world. People who have never put effort into writing have no idea how vulnerable you feel after you've created something. Remember, it's easier to criticize than create. At some point, someone will make you feel like your beautiful baby is UGLY.

They might even try to pass it off as constructive criticism, "You know, I like the part about you growing up in Pittsburgh. I thought all your talk about working at the steel company was boring though." This will feel like a knife to your heart, and I just want you to say to yourself, "Carla told me someone would tell me my baby is ugly and it doesn't matter!"

Exercise #5 Make a Preservation Plan

What physical form would you like for stories?
- Digital file you can email
- Short, written stories you can pass around at a family gathering
- A bound collection of stories
- A video or audio recording

One of the best ways to enlarge the impact of your stories is to make sure they survive for future generations. Once you write a story or identify some important photos, how can you increase the odds that they won't be lost? What kinds of backups (or copies) can you create?

With whom can you share copies of your stories and photos? Family? Organizations? (Keep in mind that physical space can be an obstacle, so digital copies may be better received.)

Can you think of a good time to share your work? A specific holiday, special occasion or family gathering?

If you have a will, does it address who can have access to your digital content and passwords?

6

Wash, Rinse, Adapt, Repeat

C – Context
A – Account
R – Reflect
E – Enlarge

That's it. The four steps of CARE can be applied over and over to as many stories as you can tell. The goal now is to imagine how you might incorporate a practice of telling your family stories into your life. Some people like to set aside a few months and work on it as a project. They stop for a while and come back to it. Others like to build it into their weekly routine. For example, I often wake up on Sunday morning and spend an hour writing my own stories. One woman I know set up a weekly call each Sunday morning with her mom, and they worked from a list of prompts to talk about her mom's life and the family history. Her mom appreciated having time to think through the questions ahead of time so she could gather information and photos.

Psychologically, we know we are more likely to continue habits that feel good. After you've written a couple short LifeSketches, I want you to reflect on the process. What did you like, what didn't you like? There can be a wide range of responses to this process.

You might be surprised at the ways you can alter the process to focus more

on what you enjoy and less on what you don't. For example, many people are motivated
when they are working with others. I am writing this in the midst of the COVID
pandemic, and the most introverted people I know are starved for human contact.
Recording family memories can definitely be structured to be a relational exercise.

There are lots of ways to work together. You can interview each other; you can read stories
to each other. You may just realize you do not like sitting alone at a computer. So, you are
someone who may opt to have a friend interview you and make an audio recording of the
interview. Reflect on the parts you don't like and see if you can find ways to work around
them.

What did you NOT enjoy about the process?

What did you enjoy about creating a LifeSketch?

Identify Your Purpose

You had a reason for picking up this book. What was it? It's easier to keep doing
something if you are clear on your purpose for doing it. Your motivations may evolve, too.
When I started writing, my motivation was an internal drive to process the grief of losing
my parents. Now, I have two motivations for writing family history. First, I want my kids
to see themselves as part of a bigger story. Second, I want to celebrate and memorialize
some family members who are no longer alive.

Other reasons people value telling family stories:

Celebrate ethnic heritage

Share religious tradition
Pass down stories your grandparents told
Connect your family to local, national or world history
Recognize accomplishments or artisanship in the family
Honor ancestors for the obstacles they overcame to make your life possible

Being clear on your purpose can also help if you feel stuck working on a project. Sometimes we get stuck because we start writing a story that doesn't end up reflecting the unspoken goals we had for the project. We may need to stop writing that story and start writing a different one.

Dealing with Discouragement

If you've ever tried to share something you've written and gotten a negative or disinterested reaction, it can be quite dispiriting. After all, it takes effort to write a story or organize and label family photographs. Rejecting what I've created is painfully close to rejecting me. It's important to remember that the reactions you receive may not have anything to do with what you created.

Surprisingly, people can have strong reactions to the idea of family history. When people ask me about my job, I tell them that I help people record their family history. Since that is not a particularly common profession, it takes a minute for people to process it. At that moment, I often find myself involuntarily holding my breath.

Sometimes, their face lights up and they say, "Oh that's so interesting!" (Whew! Exhale.) Sometimes, they get a scowl on their face and whatever they say always seems to start with "Pff" followed by something like "no interesting people in my family; they were all poor coal miners." Or "sounds boring, like history class." Or "oh," (eye roll) "you should talk to my cousin Glenda. She loves that stuff."

Some people have absolutely no interest in family history. Hard to imagine, if you're someone who loves it! But I've learned to smile and say, "Yeah. Some people find it fascinating and some people find it boring." And I shrug. So, here's my advice: LEARN TO SHRUG when people show no interest in your stories or photographs.

For some people, there are deeply painful associations with family. One friend's mom was seriously mentally ill with schizophrenia and she would often forget to feed her son for days. He learned to climb on the counters at the age of 3 and scour through the cabinets for food. Many people have fathers who abandoned the family or mothers who had a drug addiction. There are a million reasons someone may not want to talk or even think about family that have absolutely nothing to do with you.

For others, they simply have other interests that don't include family history. A colleague of mine organizes marathons. I work hard to stay active, but I have a long-standing disdain for jogging. I could give you a long list of reasons why, including my complete lack of athleticism and a very mean gym teacher in elementary school. But my colleague also has a rich network of friends and contacts because marathoners have their own little community. I've learned to appreciate the people and the culture from a distance but running is just not one of my interests.

I worked with a client recently to self-publish his family history. It was an ambitious undertaking because he came from a long line of public servants and military leaders who had interesting, well-documented lives. We ended up with a beautiful 200-page book in full color. I saw him a few weeks after we finished the project and I asked him if he'd shared his book with family members. His shoulders slumped as he said, "Yes, but they didn't seem very impressed."

It's difficult to continue to put effort into something without some positive support from those around you. You may wonder why you should bother to write about your life if nobody cares. The truth is, you are not writing for *nobody,* you are writing for that *somebody* who does care and you may not know who that is yet.

It's About Timing

When my father retired from a career as a physicist with the U.S. Army, he took up writing his memoir. The family was surprised. He'd had secretaries throughout his professional career and didn't know how to type. He was an undiagnosed dyslexic whose handwriting and spelling were notoriously atrocious. It was not an easy undertaking for him, but he wrote his account of growing up in Depression-era Virginia.

When he finished, he went to an office supply store and had them make copies and bind them. I am horrified to admit this, but I did not read his story. I had just graduated from college and I was busy trying to build a career. At one point, when he was still teaching himself to type, he gave me some pages and asked me to type them up. I already had a job in publishing so I assumed I was qualified to do some light editing as I typed. He got angry with me and the whole topic of his writing became a sore subject for a long time.

Fast forward 30 years and self-publishing his memoir was the way I worked through my grief after he died. The same story I got in a tiff with him about eventually became one of the most meaningful things in my life.

My observation is that most families develop at least one person in a generation that cares for family history. Sometimes it's not the person you expect and sometimes they don't become interested until later in life. After all, the significance of family stories becomes much clearer once you are old enough not to take them for granted.

Your job is to leave a trail of breadcrumbs for the next generation. Remember, there are many writers and artists who were ignored when they were alive and only became well known much later. Some art needs to age before people see the significance.

His-story/Her-story

My major in grad school was history. (I'm sure you are *shocked!*) My favorite class wasn't a history class; it was a class about how history is recorded called Historiography. What we think of as "history" is really only a tiny portion of what happened in the past. It's the portion that got written down. For most of history, that limited the stories we collected because only a small subset of people had the education, resources and leisure time to write. What has passed as the official story of humanity was actually the written accounts of only the wealthy and the powerful.

Eventually, a movement within the field of history began to switch attention from the wealthy to the largest part of every population – the average citizen or worker. Suddenly, things that weren't viewed as having any historical significance – like the everyday life of serfs, journals written by women, etc. – became crucial to the official account of history.

Whatever your daily life consists of is an important window into a time and into the life of a family and its descendants. I'm confident Anne Frank did not anticipate the reach of her teenage journal when she first put pen to page. The reaction you get today (especially from young people) is not an indication of the value of what you've created.

One of my favorite graduate professors had a plaque on her office wall that I reflect on often. It said:

Rules of Life
1. Show Up
2. Pay Attention
3. Tell the Truth
4. Don't get too Attached to the Results

It's nearly impossible not to be attached to the stories you have carefully taken time to record. But trust in the value of them, even if others don't see it right away. You are adding to history.

Celebrate Every Step

It's important you find ways to celebrate your own efforts. For me, it usually involves chocolate-covered almonds and a leisurely stroll in the park. Give some thought to what little rituals make you feel like you've given yourself a pat on the back.

Also, you never need to feel bad about what you don't get done with LifeSketch. If you take down a box of photos and label them, that's great! If you write a story, fantastic! Did you reach out to an older relative to ask questions, wonderful! No one ever tells all their stories. Every step you take helps connect all the people before you to all the people after you.

Summary

Everything that is meaningful is hard – at least some of the time. So, look for ways to make the process more enjoyable by adapting how you do it and whom you do it with. Be clear on your purpose for writing stories. That will help you weather any disinterested or negative responses to your work. Look for ways to build little family history rituals into your life – whether it is time writing, time on the phone with older relatives, or time-sharing stories with your grandkids. If all you do is keep working on the steps of CARE through multiple family stories, you have made a fabulous contribution to your family story!

Once you're comfortable with the basic steps, the following chapters will show you how to improve the accuracy of your stories through research and the quality of your stories through better writing. It's ok to skim these sections and pick just one area to focus on the next time you sit down to write a story. The next chapters are intended for beginning researchers and writers, so if you have a lot of experience in either area you may want to skip ahead.

Done is better than perfect.

Exercise #6

What is your purpose or hope in telling family stories?

The LifeSketch process is simple, but it's not always easy. We all have challenges to overcome in the process. My guess is that you know yourself well enough to know where the obstacles might arise. Finding time, distraction, not remembering enough details, you can't type…

What do you expect will be your obstacles?

What would help you manage those obstacles?

7

Develop Your Writing Skills

How did you feel about writing assignments in high school? (That's not rhetorical, take a moment and think about it....)

I guarantee whatever you felt, there is a part of you that relives those feelings when you're writing family history. If you got praise from your teachers, you may have good associations. If you were traumatized by papers returned to you with so much red ink, they looked like stop signs from a distance, then you may feel anxious or discouraged. Here is the great thing about being an adult: You don't have to please anyone but yourself with your writing.

I enjoyed reading and writing in English class. However, when I remember the grammar quizzes and sentence diagraming, my heart races, my skin feels itchy and I have the urge to request a bathroom pass. One of my challenges was that I was never convinced that what I was being taught had any serious benefit to me. When you become an adult, you have the ability to connect specific skills to outcomes YOU want – not to a grade or pleasing a teacher.

Most of us who take the time to write stories want the people who read them to 1) understand them and 2) enjoy them. Writing is just a tool. Like a hammer. Or a drill. The more skilled you become at using this tool, the easier it is for people to understand the information, and the more likely they will enjoy the stories...and KEEP reading.

So, even if you have bad associations with writing, focus on the goal every writer wants: You want people to read your stories. Your stories and experiences deserve to be recorded whether or not you consider yourself a good writer. And your goal, like most professional writers, is to work at being a little bit better writer than you were last week.

If you've always had a secret desire to write the great American novel, there are many online and published resources to develop your skills. For the purpose of writing family history, I want to focus on a few simple, specific tips that help you draw in your readers with more active and interesting writing.

Use Strong Language (Swearing, optional)

Ever think about how much we are discouraged from using strong language in day-to-day life? Toning down your language is often praised for being tactful and it can avoid heated arguments. The only two places where we are often asked to use strong language is in public speaking and writing. If that's not something you do regularly, you probably haven't thought much about what makes your words powerful.

Make Your Verbs Grunt

I worked at a college that offered free use of the school's gym to employees. The fall was always an entertaining time at the gym because that's when the football team spent part of every practice lifting weights. I'd be taking my middle-aged lady stroll on the treadmill, and every few minutes guttural, animalistic sounds would erupt from across the room followed by a loud BANG of weights dropping to the floor. I was startled every time. I always had the urge to grab a five-pound weight and make as much noise as I could as I fought to lift it off the ground. You want your verbs to work like football players, you want them to carry a lot of weight.

Strong writing uses descriptive verbs. Verbs tell us about actions, so make the words that describe actions interesting. Let's take a simple example of the verb: to walk. Walking has a low-energy vibe that doesn't create much of a picture.   Depending on the context, think of all the more interesting words you could use:

Stomp
Plod
Mope
Shuffle
Saunter
Trudge

Ramble

Stride

Amble

She walked across the room and sat in a chair.

vs.

She moped across the room and plopped down in a chair.

The second sentence creates a much more vivid and interesting picture in your mind. It generates questions like, *Why is she moping? Is she OK?* Those unconscious questions are what drive readers to keep reading.

Of all verbs in the English language, one verb rises above all others in its capacity to put readers to sleep! In English class they called it the verb "to be," but it includes all of the words listed below.

Be

Being

Been

Am

Is

Are

Was

Were

Don't forget contractions that contain these words like

I'm

We're

They're

He's/She's

When Hamlet wonders whether "To be or not to be?" he emanates existential angst about the trials and tribulations of life. But most of the time, the verb carries no such drama.

Verbs tell us about the action taking place. Strong verbs usually tell us HOW the action is taking place. In the example above, I can walk across the room – but how did I walk? I moped across the room.

In Chapter 5, I paraphrased a fascinating letter written by a WWII bomber pilot about a mission he flew over Berlin. His writing was excellent, but let's just lift one sentence out of his original account and see if we can punch it up by answering HOW the action took place. Prior to this sentence, the plane had been hit by enemy fire and had lost two engines.

My co-pilot and I <u>were so busy</u>, that this all <u>was</u> like a dream.

vs.

My co-pilot and I worked frantically to stabilize the plane and avoid incoming flak. Our movements so automatic and instinctive, they felt like a dream.

Two things I want to point out about this second sentence. First removing the verb "to be" usually requires restructuring the sentence. This means you can't go through your story and just erase "to be" verbs and add a different verb. You usually have to change the structure of the sentence. Second, the words I added explained the action "were so busy." HOW was he busy? Was he filing his nails? No, he was trying to stabilize the plane.

Give "-ing" Words the Side Eye

One more down-and-dirty trick to improve your writing is to be cautious when you use words that end with "-ing." Without getting into words that make me itch like participle and gerund, "-ing" words are often a symptom of weak verbs – often the verb "to be"

I am running every day.

vs.

I run daily.

You don't need to avoid -ing words completely. They have valid uses, but I can guarantee if you look through a piece you've written and remove some of the -ing words, you're writing will improve.

When you use "to be" and "-ing" words carefully, it will automatically help you write in what your English teacher called *active voice.* All that means is that the subject of your sentence does something (acts) as opposed to be acted upon.

Active Voice: Elephants eat peanuts.
Passive Voice: Peanuts are eaten by elephants.

You can compare the tips in this chapter to purifying gold. You raise the heat in your writing through strong, active language and it melts away the dross of ineffective, boring language.

Exercise #7

If you've been skipping exercises in the book, I won't tell, but I really want you to do this one. If you get nothing out of this book but this one point, you are on track to being a stronger writer.

1. Choose 2-3 paragraphs from one of your family stories.
2. Highlight or underline all the verbs. Every sentence should have at least one.
3. Pick a couple of verbs from each paragraph and replace them with more descriptive, active verbs. In many cases, you can change just a few words. If you used "to be" extensively you may need to rewrite some sentences.

Exercises and Notes
(Relax. You Can't Get It Wrong)

Dear Past, Thanks for the Lessons....

8

How to Tell a Good Story

We all know that similar plots can be boring or fascinating solely based on how the story is told. In 1988 Tom Hanks starred in the movie *Big* about a boy who gets his wish granted to be an adult. That same year, a movie with a very similar plot called *Vice Versa* was released. Most of us only remember one of those movies.

In the context of family history, it's important not to bend the facts for the sake of good story telling. That's a common pitfall of Hollywood movies based on real events. But there are some tried and true ways to tell stories that tend to hold readers' attention.

Sometimes they are referred to as common *plots*. But in the context of family history, we are not creating the story, we're just looking for effective ways to organize the facts in a story to make it more interesting. So, I like to think of them as story *containers*.

When you are dealing with a real person or a real-life event, there will always be lots of extraneous facts and details you know. A container – let's say for example, a suitcase – can only fit so many items of clothing. Packing a suitcase forces you to make decisions based on what you need and what can fit in the bag. For example, if you want to tell a rags to riches story about an immigrant family member, you may not include some extraneous details such as his love of photography or baseball. You can write a different LifeSketch about interesting items you leave out.

Story containers also help define a beginning, middle and end to your story, which readers will find satisfying.

Some common story plots or containers include

- Overcoming the Monster – classic underdog; giving voice to the voiceless (e.g., David and Goliath, *Jaws*, James Bond)
- Rebirth – stories of renewal; return to former glory (e.g., *A Christmas Carol, The Grinch who Stole Christmas*)
- Quest – difficult journey to obtain something of value (e.g., *Lord of the Rings, Indiana Jones*)
- Voyage and Return – transformation through travel and return (e.g., *The Wizard of Oz, Finding Nemo*)
- Rags to Riches (e.g., *Cinderella, The Man in the Iron Mask*)
- Tragedy – hero is brought down by his or her own flaws (e.g., *The Great Gatsby, The Hunger Games*)
- Comedy – the wonderfully ridiculous side of humanity (e.g., *Bridget Jones's Diary, Four Weddings and a Funeral*)

Take a minute and list the events you want to cover in a short LifeSketch. Then ask yourself if reality mirrors any of the story structures above. If it does, then that will help guide the way you tell the story, including what facts to include and what facts you set aside for a different story. Stories are intrinsically more satisfying if there is a sense of movement – starting somewhere and ending somewhere else.

Outline Your Story

Once you have a list and put items in the order you want to write about them, you have created an outline. Outlines almost instantly improve your writing for many reasons.

- You think before you write (always a good idea)
- You define a beginning, middle, and end to your story
- You create a roadmap to follow so you don't end up writing a lot of material that ends up in the trash (saving time and energy)
- You can think critically about what the best order is to tell those events (hint: it's usually not chronologically – more on this later)

Once you start using simple outlines, you'll find it difficult to write without them. It will feel like trying to drive blindfolded.

In order to create a helpful outline, start by making a list of everything you know (or everything you plan to share) about a person or event. For example, here are some facts about my grandmother Lottie. These facts are more or less in chronological order, but yours don't have to be. This is intended to be the brain dump of what you want to write about.

1. Lottie Catherine Whitacre was born in 1898 in Virginia.
2. She was the fifth child of six.
3. Her father died when she was 11.
4. Her oldest brother worked to support the family.
5. Within in a year after her father died, her oldest brother drowned, leaving the family with no income.
6. Lottie's mother was forced to remarry and place her children into other homes as servants.
7. Lottie was 12 years old when she had to go live with another family as a servant.
8. Her brother's drowning had a lasting impact on her. She had a lifelong fear of the water.
9. Lottie married at the age of 16 and was married for 40 years.
10. She gardened, canned, raised chickens, butchered and bartered to keep her family fed through the Great Depression.

Depending on where I would like my focus to be, I can pick one of several story containers that match the actual facts of her life. She had no shortage of adversity. I am drawn to the "Rebirth" or "Journey and Return" story structures. First, Lottie had a family, then she lost her family, and then she created a new family.

Pick an Interesting Point to Begin

The temptation with family history is to start at the beginning:

Lottie DeHaven was born in Virginia in 1898....

That is an important fact that I want to include, but it's not the most interesting fact. I know from a newspaper article a little bit about the night her brother drowned. Lottie's mother collapsed when she was told the news of her son's drowning. What if I started with some drama associated with that tragedy?

> *Lottie awoke to a thud and the murmurings of concerned, hushed voices. Rising from bed, she cracked open her door and peered out into the parlor. Two men helped Mother off of the floor and set her gently on her chair. Lottie's stomach felt queasy. Something was very wrong.*

As we discussed earlier, this type of opening poses questions in the reader's mind. When the reader has questions, they keep reading. That's what you want!

Get in Trouble

If you are old enough to read this book, I have no doubt that you've experienced what is at the core of all good stories: adversity. Take a minute to think about the last movie or TV show you watched. What was the conflict? It may have been a problem, an obstacle, an enemy, that the main character had to address.

If you can choose a central conflict around which to tell your relative's story, you can use some tools out of the professional writer's toolbox to make your story engaging. This may seem challenging at first, but you've got one thing going for you: every person that ever lived has faced a big problem.

My grandmother's story will have more of an impact on the reader if I can organize the actual facts around a central conflict. I can focus on how my grandmother survived the loss of her family.

Show, Don't Tell

In my suggested opening for my story about Lottie, I could have simply told you that Lottie's mother was upset. But by painting a picture with actions, I've made it easier for the reader to connect with the pain the family is experiencing.

"Show, Don't Tell" is a standard and valuable tip for improving your writing. But in the context of family history, you can't always do this without inventing actions and thoughts that you can't know from looking at research documents. In this case, I had several newspaper articles about her brother's drowning that gave me some details to work with. Even with that, I still ad-libbed Lottie's reaction by saying her stomach was queasy. I don't actually know that. But it is a small detail that helps readers relate to Lottie. You will have to decide what liberties you want to take in an effort to "show, don't tell." My recommendation is to use ad-libbed details sparingly.

You do have the option of writing historical fiction about your relative. To do this, you will make up all kinds of actions and details but stick with the broad outline of events in your relative's life. The difference is that you are clear with your reader that the work is fiction.

The ultimate "show" in family history is photographs and other visual aids. Pictures can be powerful. There are few experiences like looking at a photograph of a great grandparent you never met. It can evoke intense curiosity, awe, sadness and a deep sense of connection.

Visual aids have also become the norm for younger generations. If they want to learn something new, they are far less likely to reach for a book than they are to search for a YouTube video. If you've ever had trouble fixing things around your house, you probably know how valuable a YouTube video or DIY TV show can be. When we're sharing our family stories with kids, our main competition is not books, it's video. The more visually interesting you make your stories, the more likely you will engage all readers – especially younger readers.

Photos can be an important part of telling our family story. In Chapter 10, we'll talk more about caring for and sharing family photographs.

1. Create a list of all of the facts about the character or event you want to write about. It can be as long or as short as you like but try to get at least six facts.
2. Identify key challenges your character faced. Which one or two seem the most important or impactful to what happened in his or her life?
3. Identify concrete actions that you know happened in their story. For example, did they leave their hometown and travel to a port city to immigrate to the U.S.? Were they a passenger in steerage on a ship? Did they travel to France to fight in the war?
4. Choose an interesting place to start your story. Remember, it doesn't have to be in chronological order. You are trying to grab your reader.
5. Make a list of emotions your character may have felt when you look at the events in your list – pride, sadness, excitement, fear, etc. Think about where you can bring out those emotions in your story.
6. Make your outline. All this means is to put your list in order of where you're going to start, what the middle or climax will be, and where your story will end.
7. Make it visual – add photos, maps, etc.

Exercises and Notes

(Relax. You Can't Get It Wrong)

Don't be afraid to fail. Be afraid not to try.

9

Develop as a Family Historian

The most important contribution you can make to the next generation is to pass on what you know about your family. What you've been able to write so far of your family history is probably your own experiences or the family stories you were told. If that's all you do, that is a fabulous contribution to your family story.

But what about what you don't know? Or what if you have an inkling that some of what you were told isn't true?

Once you start asking these questions, you are beginning the process of family research. **Solid family history research requires you to start with the present and work backwards in time.**

Sometimes families have ideas about famous people they might be related to. My mother-in-law's maiden name is Cyrus. At every family reunion, someone asks me if they are related to Billy Ray Cyrus or Miley Cyrus. What's important here is that you don't start your research with the famous person. You start with yourself. (If you're wondering, I still don't know if they are related to Miley).

If you want to begin to follow the knowable facts back in time, imagine you are building a set of stairs from the bottom up. The first step is you. List your basic information:

Name at birth
Birthdate
Birth location
Mother
Father

Next, list the same basic information for your parents and then your grandparents, and so on. Once you start recording details for people who have died, you'll want to list where they lived when they died.

Name at birth
Birthdate
Birth location
Death date
Death location
Name of Mother
Name of Father

Some people will not be able to provide basic family information past their own parents. That's where family history research skills can help.

Mystery Family Members

For many people there are significant holes in their family tree. Adoptees may have little to no information about their biological parents. You may have a single mother in your tree and not have the identity of the father. Many African Americans run into what Dr. Henry Louis Gates terms, "the brick wall of slavery." In this situation families were not given the dignity of being recorded by name, so there is a very limited paper trail available. In this case, you will need to develop your research skills (tips to follow) or hire someone who can help you identify your mystery person/people.

The advancement of DNA technology makes it increasingly likely that some of these mysteries will be solved. A friend whose mother was adopted wanted to know more about her biological maternal line. All we had to work with was an Ancestry.com DNA kit and a redacted copy of her mother's original birth certificate. My friend's mother was willing to submit a DNA test and in about six months we were able to identify both mystery parents.

If you decide to use DNA to help discover a mystery family member, be aware that it is not as simple as spitting in a tube and getting a letter with the answer you seek. It can be a long process of tracking down people who show up as DNA matches to you and comparing their DNA matches to your DNA matches until the process of elimination gives you a few likely candidates. At that point, you often need the assistance of a biological family member to help you get a final answer.

In the case of my friend, we were lucky enough to find a biological cousin who was willing to help with our research. Though we were able to identify both biological parents, only one parent has agreed to have contact so far. But we were still able to identify a simple family tree for the parent who denied contact that went back several generations. *If you are biologically related, you have the right to your own DNA information, whether or not you have a relationship.*

If you are just starting to learn how to do genealogical research, don't start with your mystery person. Develop your skills on branches of the family that are known or even your adopted family tree.

Seek Original Records

Birth, death and marriage certificates are referred to as "Vital Records" and they often contain the information you need to keep building your staircase. For some of you, this is where you lose interest. That's fine. You can skip to the next chapter. Records research is not for everyone.

ProTip: The spelling of your family name may vary in official records. When literacy was not always guaranteed, spelling a name the way it sounded was considered acceptable. In some cases where a records clerk filled out forms for people, language barriers created more confusion in records. Try to verify other facts, such as birthdate or address to confirm if this is the family member you seek – regardless of spelling.

I spend several hours every week searching through digital records. I wouldn't say I like searching records, but you know what I like? Getting answers!

I currently have a client who wants to know where in Europe her family lived before they immigrated to the United States. She had a vague sense it was Eastern Europe, but that's all she knew. How did we answer that question? Vital records. We were able to locate a marriage record for her grandparents that listed where they were born: Lithuania. We were able to find additional records, such as her grandfather's WWII registration card to corroborate the information.

Now if you'd rather stick a finger in your eye than spend hours searching for records, you are not alone. You can always hire a genealogist to search for you or become really good friends with someone whose idea of a fun Friday night is to pour a glass of wine and play around on Ancestry.com. When I first started building my family tree, I often ran into information about my family members that had been posted online by the same person. I didn't recognize her username. I finally sent her an email and told her it looked like we were researching some of the same people and wondered if we were cousins. Turns out, it was a friend of my sister who loves to build trees for her friends for fun. My sister and I now jokingly refer to her as "Cousin Katie."

If you are willing to build your research skills, you are fortunate to be doing family history in a time when so many records are digitized – and millions of new records are being added each year. It's possible you can find, for example, your grandparents birth or marriage certificates online.

Websites such as Ancestry.com and FamilySearch.org are designed specifically for this purpose. Some websites, such as Ancestry.com, require an annual membership. However, many public libraries allow you to use the website for free while in the library building. FamilySearch.org is free, but it can be harder than Ancestry to search. You have to weigh your interest in learning more advanced research skills, the ease of finding what you want and how much money you want to spend. The records on the various genealogy websites are not identical, but there is a lot of overlap. For example, all of the major genealogy websites give you access to publicly available federal census records.

No National Record Keeping System

Unfortunately for family historians, many countries, including the U.S., have no national system for collecting vital records. In the U.S., records are collected and organized by the county or state in which your family member lived. The challenge with this system is that every location can determine the terms by which they make these documents available. So, you will have to investigate the counties where your family lived to find out their rules.

This is one reason I encourage you to make friends with other family historians. A five-minute conversation with someone who has done research in the same area can save you hours of work and effort.

Common rules that are established by states and counties involve who can get access to records and when. You need to find out things such as

1. How old does a document have to be before it's public? These rules are intended to protect the privacy of the living. Often the number of years is different based on the type of document. In my area, I can view birth certificates that are 75 years old, but death certificates are open to the public after 20 years.
2. Have the records been digitized? If so, where are they available?
3. If the record is not digitized, can you order a copy from the county or state? There is usually a fee of anywhere between $12 and $25 to get copies. You'll also want to know if they return the fee if they can't find your document.
4. Are there documents missing? Some areas may have had a fire or flood that wiped out old paper documents. Chicago, for example, has no vital records prior to the The Great Chicago Fire of 1871.

Simple internet searches for "vital records genealogy" and the county and state often tell you what you need to know. For example, "Cook County Illinois Vital Records Genealogy" will show me several options for finding Chicago vital records. All of the major genealogy websites will be listed, but so will the county and state offices that hold the original records. Be sure to include "genealogy" in your search, because counties often have a separate website for people who are trying to get certified copies of their own birth or wedding certificates for official purposes like obtaining a passport. Genealogy requests are usually handled by a different office.

Another great resource is FamilySearch.org Wiki. If you type the location you want to know about in the search bar, it will provide a page of information about family research specifically for that location.

When all else fails, call the county clerk's office and ask. If you don't get a helpful answer, try back another day and see if someone else can be more helpful.

International Records

If your family has immigrated in recent generations, you will quickly need to research records in another country. Many international records are available online. Often, a necessary step in international research is to determine the hometown where your relative lived. This information is often found on naturalization (citizenship) records or military records such as WWII registration cards. Once you know the town, you can begin to research where the vital records are kept for that area and whether they have been digitized. Be aware that records may no longer exist if war, fire or flood has claimed them.

The ease of finding international records varies dramatically from one country to the next. Sometimes a simple search on a genealogy website will pull up records for you. Sometimes you will need to write or email the local government where the records are kept and ask about the steps you need to take.

My best tip for new researchers is to find other people who are doing research in the same country and ask for advice. There are many online groups you can join that are focused on genealogy in specific countries. There are some fabulous Facebook groups that have helped me learn the ropes for various countries where I needed to find records.

What Original Records Can Tell You

What information can be found on vital records will vary depending on the date and location. Sometimes marriage applications list the name of the bride and groom's parents, sometimes they don't. So, pack your patience and learn to enjoy the process of searching. Most family history researchers will tell you there can be a lot of time spent that feels unproductive – time *not* finding the information you seek. But when you have that "AHA" experience of finding exactly what you need to know, it can be euphoric.

Don't Trust Everything You Read

Original Documents are valuable but they are not always accurate. For example, census records can be a rich source of information, but **the accuracy of the information is only as good as the source** who spoke with the census taker. If the census taker knocks on a door in 1920, he is going to get his information from whoever answers the door. It might be a 14-year-old child, or an aunt that lives with the family. If no one answers the door, he might even get information from the next-door neighbor. This is why it is ideal to have more than one source of information whenever possible.

Similarly, when you look at death certificates, notice who is listed as the source. Is it the wife? The child? The son-in-law? The information is only as good as the source. And even if the source is credible, you must consider other factors such as emotional distress and language barriers.

I recently requested a death certificate for a client and it listed the wrong birthday and the wrong names for his parents. The source was credible – it was his wife – but the family had only recently immigrated, and she only spoke Polish. Her husband had died suddenly in a work-related accident, so she must have been deeply distressed.   While I still got some useful information from the document, such as the date of death and the cause of death, I had to look at multiple records to be able to determine his birth date and his parents' names.

Beyond Vital Records

Depending on your family history, there are several other types of records that can provide a wealth of family history information. The three most notable are immigration records, military records, and religious records.

If you have an ancestor who immigrated from another country, they may have filled out paperwork to become a U.S. citizen. The information provided on these forms will vary depending on the date because the forms evolved to ask more questions over time. Naturalization forms from the first half of the 20th century can offer a treasure trove of family history information. They can list parents' names, the immigrant's town of birth, a list of their children with birthdates, etc. Occasionally, I even find a picture of the applicant attached to the paperwork! (See Figure 4 on p. 88)

Another related set of documents is passenger lists that show the names of people who traveled to and from the United States. Ellis Island opened in 1892 and many of those records are available for free online. You are able to search by name, but you will want to try to find ways to verify that a "John Smith" you find in a name search is YOUR John Smith. Sometimes you can verify this by seeing the family members they traveled with or by comparing the date of your passenger list with other information that supports the specific year of arrival.

Honest research allows you to admit what you don't know. I have found several immigration records that I have not been able to prove is the person I am researching. If the person traveled alone and had a common name, it can be difficult to be sure. That's OK. Just be clear that such records are clearly labeled as unverified. Later research may help you find out for sure.

Family researchers can often find a lot of information in the records kept by the family's religious community. Synagogues, churches, and mosques can be wonderful repositories for birth, marriage, and death records. Committed groups of genealogists and historians have developed vital record databases based on location and religion. For example, JRI-Poland.org is dedicated to Jewish records from Poland. Arkivdigital.net has the largest collection of Swedish church records. Some of these websites require a subscription, but often libraries or cultural museums will allow you free access if you are researching on the premises. FamilySearch.org is a wonderful (and free) resource for many church records, but it takes a little work to learn how to use their online catalog.

How Many Stairs in your Staircase?

There are many obstacles that can limit the number of steps (generations) you can trace your family. It's important to remember that **you can't skip steps**. If you are unsure – for example – who were the parents of your grandparents, you must stop building your staircase in that family line until you resolve that issue. You can hypothesize based on available information, but until you prove your hypothesis you may find yourself accidently researching someone else's family!

This is the biggest mistake new family history researchers make. You are not a "good" family history researcher if you can build a family tree that goes back to Charlemagne. You are good at family research if you are confident that each step in your staircase is built on a solid foundation of facts. You're a good family researcher when you admit what you don't know. You're a good family researcher when you seek out the expertise of others.

This is your genealogical brick wall. It is intrinsic to family history. Unless you can track your family back to Adam and Eve, all of us hit brick walls eventually. There are lots of tricks for breaking through brick walls that we won't cover here. The most important thing at this point is for you to recognize when you've hit one and stop.

TRIPLICATE   No. 102863

UNITED STATES OF AMERICA

DECLARATION OF INTENTION
(Invalid for all purposes seven years after the date hereof)

Eastern District of Michigan | *In the* _________________ District _________ *Court*
ss:
Southern Division | *of* the United States *at* Detroit, Mich.

I, _____ Sven Emanuel Strom _____
(Full true name, without abbreviation, and any other name which has been used, must appear here)
now residing at ___ 1341 Putnam Ave., Detroit, Wayne, Mich. ___
(Number and street) (City or town) (County) (State)
occupation ___ shoe maker ___, aged __ 48 __ years, do declare on oath that my personal description is:
Sex __ male __, color __ white __, complexion __ medium __, color of eyes blue
color of hair _____ black, height __ 5 __ feet 9½ __ inches; weight __ 172 __ pounds; visible distinctive marks
_____ none
race _____ Scandinavian _____; nationality Swedish
I was born in ___ Sundsvall, Sweden ___, on ___ Sept. 16, 1882
(City or town) (Country) (Month) (Day) (Year)
I am _____ married. The name of my wife or husband is _____ Ella
we were married on _____ June 5, 1905 _____, at ___ Traverse City, Mich. ___; she or he was
(Month) (Day) (Year) (State or country)
born at __ Sunne, Sweden __, on __ Oct. 1, 1881 __, entered the United States
(City or town) (State or country) (Month) (Day) (Year)
at _____ New York, N.Y. _____, on ___ Sept. 1882 ___, for permanent residence therein, and now
(City or town) (State) (Month) (Day) (Year)
resides at ___ xxxxxxx Mich. ___ I have __ 4 __ children, and the name, date and place of birth,
(City or town) (State or country)
and place of residence of each of said children are as follows: Raymond 4-29-06; Martin 6-20-07
Erma 3-26-12; Anna 11-25-14; All born in Michigan, reside Detroit

I have _____ heretofore made a declaration of intention: Number 81762 _____, on __ Aug. 19, 1920
(Date)
at ___ Detroit, Mich. ___ (State) Wayne County Circuit Court (Name of court)
my last foreign residence was _____ Sundsvall, Sweden _____ (Country)
I emigrated to the United States of America from Trondhem, Norway
(City or town) (Country)
my lawful entry for permanent residence in the United States was at New York, N.Y.
(City or town) (State)
under the name of _____ Strom, Sven _____, on __ Dec. 12, 1901
(Month) (Day) (Year)
on the vessel ___ SS Teutonic ___
(If other than by vessel, state manner of arrival)
I will, before being admitted to citizenship, renounce forever all allegiance and
fidelity to any foreign prince, potentate, state, or sovereignty, and particularly,
by name, to the prince, potentate, state, or sovereignty of which I may be at
the time of admission a citizen or subject; I am not an anarchist; I am not a
polygamist nor a believer in the practice of polygamy; and it is my intention in
good faith to become a citizen of the United States of America and to reside
permanently therein; and I certify that the photograph affixed to the duplicate
and triplicate hereof is a likeness of me: So HELP ME GOD.

Sven Emanuel Strom

Sven Emanuel Strom
(Original signature of declarant without abbreviation, also alias, if used)
Subscribed and sworn to before me in the office of the Clerk of said Court,
at __ Detroit, Mich. __ this __ 28th __ day of __ Oct. __
anno Domini 19 30. Certification No 14-4385 _____ from the Commis-
sioner of Naturalization showing the lawful entry of the declarant for permanent
residence on the date stated above, has been received by me. The photograph
affixed to the duplicate and triplicate hereof is a likeness of the declarant.

Deputy *Clerk of the* ___ U.S. District ___ *Court*.

By _______________, _______ Clerk.

[SEAL]

Form 2202-L-A.
U. S. DEPARTMENT OF LABOR
NATURALIZATION SERVICE

14—2623 U. S. GOVERNMENT PRINTING OFFICE: 1929

*Figure 4: A Sample Naturalization Record. Most have helpful genealogy information, and some will
even include photographs.*

Where's the Proof?

If you develop as a family historian, you will find that you need to offer documentation to prove parts of your family story. For example, if you are writing about multiple generations, how do you know the names of great-great-grandparents?   Something like a family Bible might be a great resource, but serious researchers will try to corroborate information with multiple sources like vital records, census records, etc.

ProTip: Someone else's family tree is NOT considered proof. However, a cousin's family tree still might be helpful IF they list their sources and you check the sources yourself.

People that are new to genealogical research underestimate the importance of knowing where your information came from. When I first started, I would look at records until I became satisfied that a piece of information was fact. What I quickly learned (okay, probably not quickly enough) was that records often disagree. So, you need to know where you gleaned your information so that you can weigh the validity of sources if it's required. For example, a census record may give me the year someone immigrated. If I am able to find their naturalization paperwork and it lists a different year, which document is more credible? (Usually, it's the naturalization paperwork because I know the subject filled it out himself, unlike the census which may have gotten information from an in-law who happened to answer the door when the census taker came.)

In classic genealogical writing, a lot of the proof is included in the main text and supported by copious footnotes. One common format that calls for meticulous source citation is called Register Style and some genealogy organizations require you to write up your research in this format for it to be considered serious genealogy research. Unless your audience is genealogists, I suggest you move most of the proof documentation to an appendix or footnotes. It's boring for people who are not genealogists.

Any discussion of source citations can bring back bad memories of English class. I, for one, despised formatting all my sources in the correct order with the right punctuation. Once I started genealogy research, I began to view citations with more respect. Citing sources when you are doing your own research helps YOU. When you run into conflicting information, it helps you resolve questions because you can go back and weigh the validity of each source. So, even though I do not recommend weighing down the body of text with source citations, I want to stress that knowing where you got your information will help you in later research.

What constitutes proof? Ideally, you want two or three original documents to validate information such as the names of your great grandparents. For example, you might cite sources such as your grandmother's birth (or death) certificate, the 1910 Federal Census, and notes written in a family Bible.

The gold standard for documenting sources is Elizabeth Shown Mills's book *Evidence Explained.* It is a hefty volume that is dedicated just to writing genealogical citations. In general, here is what you need to know for each source:

Title – If it's not a book, you'll list the record source (e.g., 1850 Census, Buffalo, Erie County, New York).
Author (if applicable)
Publisher/Website – If you find, for example, a census record on Ancestry.com, you list the website as the publisher.
Location/Repository/Library
Call Number/Microfilm Number
Citation Detail (page #, image #, etc.)

Join Genealogy Groups Locally and Online

If you really want to develop your skills, one of the best things you can do is get on the email list for your local genealogy society. You may not have known you have a local genealogy group, but there is a good chance you do. I live in the suburbs of Chicago, so there are several genealogy groups that I can attend that are within a half-hour drive. In my area, most are associated with the local public libraries. They often meet there. They have speakers come and talk about better ways to do your research. Genealogy groups can form by town, county, or state. So, if you can't find one in your town, you can check nearby towns and then do an internet search for the name of your county and genealogy. There are even regional genealogy societies that focus on Midwest states or Northeast states. Once you get on their email list, you can usually tell how active they are and whether they are covering the type of information you need at this point in your journey.

My mother was raised in northeast Virginia in an area commonly called The Northern Neck. Since I live near Chicago, I can't attend meetings there, but I still ask to be on their email list. Why? Because I am researching in their area and I want to learn about the research resources in their area.

Facebook and other social media platforms have some wonderful genealogy pages you can follow. I recently wanted to hone my skills in doing Eastern European research because we have a lot of Eastern European descendants in the Chicago area who ask me to do family research. I found some absolutely fabulous groups on Facebook that focus on Polish and Eastern European genealogy. I can post questions day or night and people are often eager to share their knowledge and expertise.

Do You Have to Develop Your Research Skills?

No. I am a firm believer that everyone has a unique way to contribute to their family story. If records research is not your thing, but you have a passion for other areas like collecting and scanning family photos, interviewing relatives or writing your own stories then do that instead. Stick your toe in the water. Try to do some research and see what happens. Generally, people who are attracted to family history research figure it out pretty quickly. For people that fall in love with it, it usually happens when you really want to know the answer to a particular question so you start searching through documents and then BOOM! You find the information you were seeking and the endorphin rush kicks in. Yeah….we're nerds.

10

Preserve Stories by Protecting Photographs

Photographs are one of my favorite parts of doing family history. When I work with my clients, one of the first things I ask them after the names and dates for their parents and grandparents is "Do you have any pictures?" I love looking at the clothes, the hairstyles, and the facial expressions. Sometimes there are even clues about relationships and personalities.

Old family photographs often don't get the care they deserve. It is not unusual for me to walk into an antique shop and find a box of old black and white photos that have been given away because someone thought, *I don't know who those people are!*

Photographs can also be hard to organize and store. When I ask clients for old pictures, it is not unusual for me to get a slightly embarrassed and frustrated response something like, "Oh, they are upstairs *somewhere.*" Some people instinctively hold on to them because they have a sense that they are important but they don't know what to do with what they have.

Figure 3: My grandmother Lottie (left) and my great aunt Matilda. Include pictures with your stories whenever you can.

Where to Store Photographs

I worked in a museum that held one of C.S. Lewis's wardrobes that is believed to have been the basis for his book, *The Lion, The Witch and The Wardrobe.* I gave tours at the museum and was often asked by small children if they could climb inside. "I would really love to let you inside," I'd say in a conspiratorial whisper, "but I lost a kid in there last

month and he missed his own birthday party. I wouldn't want that to happen to you!"
Whether it is old furniture or old photographs, there are a few commonsense things – like
protecting them from toddler feet and sticky hands – you can do to preserve them for the
next generation.

**Printed photographs should be stored in locations with moderate temperature and
humidity.** They need to be stored in the same conditions where you like to live: moderate
humidity and temperatures. Attics, basements, and garages are NOT good places to store
photos because they are usually subject to wide ranges in temperature and humidity. If you
are storing photographs in a closet, pick a closet that is not adjacent to water pipes or an
outside wall.

I love the idea of displaying old family pictures around your home, but it's generally
recommended that you display copies instead of the original photographs. If you decide to
display the originals, I'd encourage you to have a digital scan made as a backup before you
put it on display. Photographs on display often fade over time.

Label Your Photographs for the Mailman

One of the experiences that motivated me to start working in family history centered on a
photograph. I spent every Christmas of my youth at my Aunt Velma's house. She passed
away before my children were born so they never had the opportunity to meet her. One
day my daughter saw a box of old belongings I was sorting and there was a picture of Aunt
Velma on the top. "Who's that?" my daughter wondered aloud. For some reason on that
particular day, it hit me hard that my daughter had no way of knowing all the treasured
relatives of my youth unless I told her.

When it's easy to identify someone in a photograph – the way I could easily identify my
Aunt Velma – it often doesn't occur to us that eventually that photo will be inherited by
someone who is not able to identify that person.

The priority families place on taking and keeping photographs varies a great deal.
Photography was a hobby in my family so we have a lot of pictures. Some families have
very few pictures. If you have too many photos to label each one, put together a "Who's
Who" box or scrapbook where you can provide a few photos of important people in your

family tree and either label the pictures directly or write information in a scrapbook next to them.

When you label your photographs, I want you to imagine you're identifying them for someone you barely know, like the mailman or the crossing guard.   The reason I say this is because you have no idea who will hold that photo (or a copy of that photo) in the future. It could be a niece or a distant cousin. Only using nicknames and relational names like grandfather, aunt, cousin, etc. may become confusing as the pictures get passed along. Be sure to include full names. If you know birth dates and locations, write those down, too. Write on the back of the photo using a soft pencil – no sharpies or ballpoint pens. Sharpies can bleed through and ruin your photo. Ballpoint pens can create indentations on your photo.

Figure 3: This 1863 picture has "Grandfather Cockrell" written on the front of the picture. Now that it has been passed down several generations, it is not immediately clear whose grandfather he is.

If you have old pictures of people you cannot identify, make photocopies and send the copies around to relatives and see if anyone can help.

Pick Favorites

If you inherit a large number of pictures or decide it's time to downsize to a smaller house, you may run into a situation where you physically cannot store photos in the proper conditions of moderate temperature and humidity.   It's important to know that even in these circumstances it is still possible to preserve your photos for posterity.

Depending on how many photographs you have, you may need to prioritize a select group for special attention. This group should certainly include old photographs that have been handed down in the family of parents, grandparents and great grandparents. It should also include a selection of pictures of the people in your immediate family at several stages of their lives. Pictures of important events, such as graduations or golden anniversaries, may make it into this group. These are the photos you definitely want to see handed down to future generations.

Once you have identified those pictures, you will want to

1. Scan them
2. Make duplicate prints
3. Give the duplicates and the originals to several different families
4. Keep a digital copy for yourself
5. Back up your digital copy

Remember all of your cousins share a set of grandparents with you. So, if you have some good photos of your grandparents, you'll want to share pictures with several other branches of the family so they can get passed down in each family tree.

This process is like the parable of the sower and the seeds. A farmer is tossing seeds in his field. Immediately, the nearby birds belly up to the bar for some dinner, so some of the seed gets eaten. Some seed survives the birds but lands on rocky soil, so it starts to grow, but then dies because there is not enough room for their roots to grow. Fortunately for the farmer, some seed lands on soft, fertile soil where their roots can go deep, and the plant grows to maturity. Your photos (and family stories) are like seeds. It's impossible to know what conditions may arise in any one family that might lead to photographs being neglected or destroyed (fires, floods, divorce, death, etc.). You want to make sure there are several copies in different families and locations so they survive to get passed down to the next generation – most importantly to that budding family historian you may not have even met yet!

Scanning photographs at home is easy once you are set up with the right equipment. Low and mid-level scanners are reasonably priced and work well for most family photos. If you are moderately tech-savvy, you may need some help getting everything set up but once the initial setup is finished, it's very easy to scan.

Determining the best settings to scan photographs is kind of like deciding if it's better to have steak or hamburgers for dinner. Of course, steak is better, but there are lots of reasons why I might opt for a hamburger tonight (money, time, convenience).

ProTip: To best preserve the quality of photographs, save them as .tiff or .png (not .jpg) files and scan at 600 dpi (dots per inch). To make those files smaller and easier to email, you can save a second version at 300 dpi as a .jpg file.

With scans, you want to have high-quality scans for preservation. These are like steak. Your high-quality scans should be saved as .tiff or .png files at 600 dpi. But you also may want a lower quality file, so they are easy to email or post online. Those are your hamburgers. Those settings can be 300 dpi, saved as a .jpg file. These files are condensed, which makes them good for email, but some detail is lost in the condensed format. The quality of .jpg files can also degrade the more times the file is opened.

When I am scanning my own photos, I generally scan them only one time at 600 dpi .tiff files. If I decide I want to email them later, I can save another copy of this same file as a .jpg file. In other words, you can turn steak into hamburger, but you can't turn hamburger into steak. So, start with scans that preserve the best quality. You can always duplicate and condense them later if the need arises.

If you are not comfortable scanning photographs yourself, you can enlist a tech-savvy relative or pay to get the photos scanned at a photography shop. If you are not doing the scanning yourself, **do not hand over all the photos at one time.** This is the equivalent to that moment in a horror movie when a character decides to check out that noise in the basement by herself. Don't do it!

Well intentioned friends or relatives may not be able to prioritize your project and pictures may get lost or damaged. If you take them into a store, try to find one that scans them on the premises. Many photography stores send photographs to other locations, increasing the chance they may get lost or damaged. By sending a few pictures at a time, no one mishap can wipe out your collection of photos.

I recommend you put together small batches that are not all the same person or time period and then wait to get those back before you turn over the next batch. This way if something happens to that batch of photographs, you haven't lost your only pictures of a particular relative.

One client did everything right. He took an old family photo to a very respectable photography store in downtown Chicago who made the scans on the premises. The day he dropped off the photo, there happened to be a protest march. That's not uncommon in a major city like Chicago. This particular protest march ended up with the photography store getting looted and his original, Civil-War era photo destroyed. Luckily, I had scanned the photograph to use in a project we worked on together so all was not lost. I am so glad he hadn't taken a big batch of photographs at one time!

Digital Fetch

One stressful day, I decided to take my dog to play fetch. There is nothing sweeter than a dog's unmitigated joy at the simple act of chasing a ball. His tail wagged, his ears perked up, and his face oozed anticipation (and a little drool). I reached back to hurl the ball as far as I possibly could, and just as I released the ball, I heard *splash!* My phone had fallen out of my pocket and into a lake.

The ease of taking pictures with our smart phones is a wonderful opportunity to record more family moments. But there are a dizzying number of apps and services that promise to back up our photographs and it's hard to understand exactly how they work and what circumstances (or settings) put your photos at risk of being lost.

Prior to my trip to the dog park, my phone service was backing up copies of my photos in the cloud. But I have a really cute dog and two lovely kids so I was taking a lot of pictures on my phone. One day, I got a notice from my phone service that my free storage was full and now they would start charging me monthly. Having just quit a job to take care of my mother, extra fees were not an option. So, I changed the settings on my phone so I would no longer be sending my photos to the cloud. When I dropped my phone in the lake, I lost about six months' worth of family pictures. The most devastating part was that my father had died in that time and my last photos with him were gone.

Today's pictures are tomorrow's family history so we need to start thinking of our phone and tablets as machines that need regular maintenance. Just like you take your car in to get the oil changed or change the batteries in a smoke detector, you need to periodically take a few steps to maintain the information and photographs on your electronic devices.

Take a moment and think about the regular maintenance you do. How do you know when it is time to get the oil changed? How do you remember to change the furnace filter? How do you remember to pay the water bill? Backing up your data needs to be considered in this same category of regular maintenance. It's hard to start new habits, so I encourage you to link this task to another habit you have already established.

In order to promote fire safety, a public service ad campaign was developed to remind people to check the batteries in their smoke detectors at the beginning and end of daylight saving time. It's a great idea because everyone is forced to deal with the annoying reality that every clock in their house now has the incorrect time. You have to break out of your regular daily routine for some maintenance. Why not push the test button on your smoke detector, too?

So, pick whatever you know will work for you and link digital maintenance to something you are already doing. Another way to think of this is that you need to schedule a regular game of digital fetch with your photos. You need to fetch them off your tablet or phone and copy them somewhere else. Tail wagging and drool, optional.

There are lots of ways to do this, but don't depend entirely on any one cloud service. You can go old-school and get the best pictures printed. Get double prints and share some copies with family members. You can download the pictures on your phone to another device, such as your computer. You can purchase thumb drives that plug directly into your phone so you can back up your photos on a thumb drive.

ProTip: Do not entrust your family photographs to one device or one app or one physical location. Multiple copies. Multiple locations. Multiple mediums. (See The Backup Rule of Three in the Appendix.)

Another safety net is a "backup" service, like Carbonite or Backblaze. A backup service periodically makes copies of everything on your computer or device and stores them on a big computer (or server) far away from your home. Note that this is different than a syncing service like Google Drive or iCloud.

Without getting too deep in the weeds, syncing services have a different primary goal than a backup service. Syncing services are designed to allow you to access the same files across multiple devices. I can start a memo on my computer at the office and finish it on my iPad sitting on my couch at home. There are times when the syncing services ability to sync files will work against your desire to preserve documents. Let's say you are trying to pull up a photograph on your iPad but you're watching TV and talking on the phone at the same time. You absent-mindedly push a few wrong buttons and delete the photograph. Depending on your app settings, a syncing service may delete the photograph across all your devices.

Your computer can crash. Your phone could end up in a lake. Your house could catch fire. Your device could get stolen. An app you're using could go out of business. When it comes to family photos, develop a habit of regular maintenance and store your photographs on more than one device and in more than one location.

Don't Just Save them, Use them!

Most of this chapter has focused on saving your photographs – old and new. But the goal of saving them is so they can be shared and enjoyed with generations to come. Display copies of old photos around the house. They are great conversation starters!

You can also use photos as a tool in gathering family history. Show a person you want to interview a photo of a relative during the interview. Photographs often unlock sensory memories that might have laid dormant without the visual prompt. You can even use pictures to prompt your own recollections.

You can create scrapbooks the old-fashioned way or by uploading pictures to a service like Shutterfly. Scrapbooks can be an alternative for people who are not interested in writing stories, but they will jot down a few facts, anecdotes, quotes or family recipes next to a picture.

Pictures are a powerful tool in engaging people with your stories. Whenever possible, include lots of pictures and visual aids into your written stories.

12

Common Problems and Questions

Where do I start?

The LifeSketch process is intended to allow you to start anywhere. You can put stories in order as you go along, but write stories that you want to write, and stories that connect to your heart. Make a few lists like Most Important Events in My Life, Things I Obsess About, etc. Most people will pick something off one of those two lists that interests them.

How do I know if anybody cares about what I'm writing?

Take the long view. The gift of age is that you know from your own experience all the things you wish you had asked older relatives but didn't. In my experience, a lot of people develop a keen interest in their family history once older loved ones begin to die. It suddenly occurs to them that they not only lost the person, but they also lost all of the family knowledge that their loved one embodied. Your writing may answer questions that family members aren't asking yet, but they will.

Can my work be picked up by a publisher?

I hope I have made the point clearly that your writing does not become important because a publisher shows interest in it. It's important to you and those who love you. All getting published proves is that a business believes it can monetize what you've written. The value of a written piece and the ability to monetize that value are best pictured on a Venn Diagram. There is overlap but they are not the same thing.

Every year one or two previously unknown authors will publish a memoir that takes the world by storm. It happens, but it is also extremely rare. In most cases the author has either been studying writing or has hired a writer to help him tell his story. Like many success stories in music and entertainment, people who look like an overnight publishing success have often spent years developing their subject area, their writing skills, or both.

If publishing interests you, by all means pursue it.

I started writing, but then I got stuck. What now?

Most of the time when people get stuck, it's because the scope of the project is too big. If your initial intent was to tell the story of your entire life, you might find that is too broad in scope. Focus on one time period or person or event. I've had many clients who want to write about several generations of their family. Some people manage to do it, but if you're stuck consider narrowing the scope. You can always add additional stories or additional generations later on.

What if I make a family member mad? What if the history is controversial?

When my father died, I put together a little video montage I wanted to play during the funeral. When I asked the funeral home about showing the video, there was an awkward silence. Finally, she said, "Yes, you can do that. But I will need you to sign something stating that you take responsibility for the content." My sister and I just looked at each other. So, I asked the obvious question, "Has this been an issue for you in the past?"

Turns out they had a funeral for a man who had been divorced. One of the children from the first marriage put together a montage of photos that included the first wife and children from the first family, but none of the second wife and her children. The second wife had a complete meltdown at the funeral. I have no idea whether this was an intentional or innocent slight, but it created quite a stir in the extended family.

Your stories and your experiences with relatives are just that: your stories. Therefore, you have the right to tell any of your stories. (This goes back to Chapter 1 when I talked about giving yourself permission to write.) However, you are wise to consider carefully with whom you want to share those stories.

I have a friend whose father left when she was young and he never worked to be a part of her life. As the father matured and remarried, he was a much better father to his second family. My friend had a difficult time hearing stories about what a great dad he was to his second family because his absence was such a huge wound in her life.

Is it wrong for the child of the second marriage to talk about his wonderful experiences with his father? Absolutely not. That is his story. But if you are aware that something is a difficult topic for another family member, proceed with caution. Seeking the advice of a counselor can be a good idea that allows you to validate your own experience while carefully discerning how and if you want to share the stories with a wider audience. This is particularly true if there is trauma, abuse, or other issues involved.

Above all, if you know the material is painful and controversial, do not attach stories to an all-family email and just shoot them out there.

There are some family stories I did not share widely before my parents died, particularly intimate details about my brother's suicide. I watched them bury their first-born child, and I did not want to open up old wounds for them. This doesn't mean I didn't write about the topic. It just means I shared those stories with a few of my closest friends and not with the entire family.

How do I record a video or audio interview with a family member?

If you are doing a virtual interview, most of the major video conferencing services will allow you to record a conversation. In some cases, the free version will not allow you to record and you have to upgrade to a paid version.

Similarly, there are apps available for both android and iOS phones that will allow you to record phone calls.

Please remember that you need to inform whoever is on an audio or video call that you are recording. Best practice is to confirm it as part of the recording. In some states it is illegal to record without consent.

If you are able to conduct an interview in person, many of the higher end smart phones have excellent video quality. You can buy a simple tripod attachment that will hold your smartphone. The biggest problem with using phones is that they don't always have enough storage to hold long videos or you might get a call in the middle of your interview. If you plan on doing a lot of interviews, it might be worth it for you to get a low to mid-level video camera. Many companies sell bundles for vlogging that will have the camera, but also include a lapel mic and an external light.

I try hard to keep my setup simple and unintimidating to my interviewees. I use a small camera and a lapel mic. If possible, I try to select locations where I can use natural light, but I occasionally add an external light. Ideally, you want your equipment to be as unobtrusive as possible to make sure your interviewee doesn't feel undue pressure. In my experience, women especially get skittish about the idea of being video recorded. I often remind them that if they could have a video recording of their grandmother, they would probably jump at the opportunity. I have had to settle for audio recordings on several occasions.

APPENDIX

Interview and/or Writing Prompts

Interview and writing prompts can help us save family stories that can't be revealed through simple vital records like birth, marriage, and death certificates. You can help save these stories by recording your own stories, or the stories of relatives.

A simple internet search for "Family History Questions" will show you a vast number of books and online resources available with suggested questions. This list is intended to give you somewhere to start. Pick the questions that interest you. How you save the answers is up to you – audio recording, video recording or written down.

1. What is the earliest home you remember? Was it an apartment, house, farm, or… ? Who lived with you?

2. What do you remember about daily life as a child? Did you have chores? (Favorite? Least favorite?)

3. In the summer, when you weren't in school, what was a day like for you? What was a day like during the school year?

4. How did you feel about school? Did you have a favorite teacher, coach or subject?

5. Did you have siblings? Tell us about your brothers and your sisters. What were your relationships like? Which sibling would you say you were closest to?

6. Did you have hobbies/activities/sports you liked to play as a kid?

7. Do you remember any particular road trip or vacation you took as a child?

8. What was your biggest challenge as a child?

9. What did you think you would do when you grew up?

10. Looking back, what do you think was wonderful about your childhood and what do you wish had been different?

11. Did you have a favorite relative or neighbor?

12. Did your family go to church or have any faith tradition? How did you feel about it?

13. How would you describe your mother (or father)? Did he/she work outside the home?

14. Did your mom or dad have favorite pastimes (cards, gardening, handiwork, bowling, etc.)?

15. Do you have any particularly good or funny memories of your mom or your dad?

16. What did your parents teach you that helped you later in life?

17. What was your first "real" job? What was your worst job? Did you have a favorite job?

18. Did any family members serve in the military? What stories did you hear about their service?

19. Did you know your grandparents? Tell about time you spent with them.

20. Did you ever hear any stories about your great-grandparents? What did you hear?

21. Did your family strongly identify with traditions from another country? If so, describe them.

22. What are you most proud of in your life?

23. What would you like your great-grandkids in the future to know about you?

The Backup Rule of Three

The Backup Rule of Three is a strategy for preserving important photos and memorabilia. A professional photographer named Peter Krogh originally developed this practice to protect his photos, but it has become the standard for many in business, archival work, and family history.

The Backup Rule of Three can be remembered with the numbers 3-2-1: 3 copies, 2 mediums, 1copy offsite.

1. Have at least three copies of your data (photos, treasured letters, videos, or audio recordings)

For example, I have this treasured old photo of the first woman in my husband's family to go to college – Addie Scales (back, right). I keep

- A physical print

- A scanned copy on my computer

- A scanned copy that is backed up *off site* by a computer back-up service like Backblaze or Carbonite (This does not include cloud syncing services like iCloud or Google Drive.)

2. Store the copies on at least two different media types

For example, I have letters my grandmother wrote my father in college. Here is my backup plan: (Still a work in progress!)

- Original letter

- Scanned letter on my computer hard drive

- Scanned letter on a thumb drive that I keep offsite (or mail to my sister).

3. Keep at least one of those copies offsite

The biggest threats to our family memorabilia tend to be water, fire, and technology failure. So, let's say your home catches fire – your physical copies and hard drive may be lost. What will be safe is the copy offsite.

Take a deep breath. None of us have ALL of our photos and memorabilia backed up three times. <u>Prioritize</u> your most important treasures first and then <u>customize</u> your plan to your needs.

If you are not tech-savvy, make at least three physical copies and send some copies to relatives you trust for safekeeping. You can also get scans done at reputable photography shops. (Look for shops that scan materials on their premises and don't send them out of the building.)

One final note on storing photos and memorabilia in your home: <u>They should be stored in the same type of environment you like to live in</u>. Attics and basements often have large temperature and humidity fluctuations that will damage your materials over time. A closet in one of your main living areas might work, but avoid areas immediately below plumbing lines and, in general, try to keep boxes at least a few inches off the floor.

There are <u>no guarantees</u>, no matter how perfectly you follow the Rule of Three. Your goal is to <u>increase your odds</u> that family treasures will be available to the next generation.

Extra Pages for Exercises and Notes

(You're doing great!)

Well done! Celebrate!

For more information on preserving your family history
follow us on Facebook at @MemoriesMatterInterviews
www.FamilyMemoriesMatter.com

For additional copies of this book, go to
our website or Amazon.com